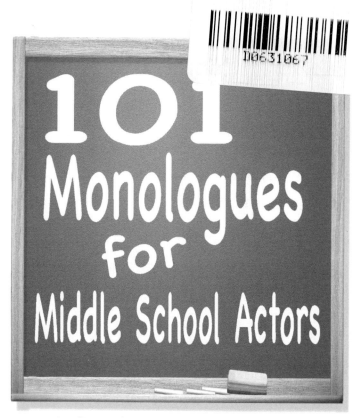

101 Monologues for Middle School Actors

Including duologues and triologues

Rebecca Young

MERIWETHER PUBLISHING LTD.
Colorado Springs, Colorado

Meriwether Publishing Ltd., Publisher
PO Box 7710
Colorado Springs, CO 80933-7710

Editor: Arthur L. Zapel
Assistant editor: Audrey Scheck
Cover design: Janice Melvin

Library of Congress Cataloging-in-Publication Data

Young, Rebecca, 1965-
   101 monologues for middle school actors: including duologues and triologues / By Rebecca Young.
   p. cm.
ISBN 978-1-56608-155-9 (pbk.)
1. Monologues. 2. Dialogues. 3. Acting. I. Title. II. Title: One hundred one monologues for middle school actors. III. Title: One hundred and one monologues for middle school actors.
   PN2080.Y66 2008
   808.82'45--dc22
                     2008018687

     1   2   3   08   09   10

Dedication

This book is dedicated to my Monday check-in friend, Marcia Jones, who helped me focus on writing fifteen minutes at a time! 101 "fifteen minutes" later, this third monologue book was born! Thanks for keeping me inspired!

Also thanks to the ones who wait patiently for those "fifteen minutes" (which tend to be much longer) to be up: Frank, Heather, Kristina, and Ashley. I love you all so much, and I couldn't do it without your support (and inspiration)! Squirrel Squad is bound to show up in a monologue sooner or later.

Thanks to all the One Voice members (past and present — you know who you are!) who remind me why I love teenage drama. So many memories ... like the one where you nasties ate the cookies that were licked and then stuck on the van windows! We'll always have Matt North and Florida, human pyramids, mattress surfing with bully Sandi (ha ha), buck buck, the circle game, and so much more! You guys keep me young.

Thanks also to my family and friends. Special thanks to Mom because she says I'm really number one — and now it's in writing, so there — Keith, MaryAnne, Dennis, Donald and Stuart! Was there really any doubt?

Of course thanks to Audrey Scheck and Art Zapel — I appreciate all that you do for me!

Lastly, Flower loves Rock.

Contents

Introduction

Middle school performers are often reluctant to jump up in front of their peers and start performing. That's why having the perfect material is a must! This book was written specifically for middle school performers — about topics they can relate to and language styles they can understand. Monologues are the perfect venue to develop vocal expression and expressive body movement. Students can choose from humorous or dramatic scenes — there is something for everyone, even the most reluctant performer!

Having a middle school daughter has kept me close to the issues at hand. Don't ever tell her I told you, but "Used Clothes, Are You Kidding Me?" was directly inspired by her! She's definitely the fashion diva of the family!

Wait until you read the triologue about the upcoming dress code. Or there's the one about the girl who has to dig through the dumpster to find her retainer — now who hasn't done that? OK, not me! But my daughter has thrown hers in the trash by accident more than once or twice.

My absolute favorite is the one about the guy in the theatre who almost kisses the wrong girl by mistake — my brother provided the inspiration for this one! (Don't ask!) If you're looking for something more serious, check out "An End and a Beginning." It's sure to bring tears to your audience's eyes. Guys will love getting "Dating Tips from King Henry" and "Cow Tipping — It's Not All Fun and Games!" and so many more!

Many of the monologues are adaptable for guys or girls — you decide! Ready to act? With 101 monologues to choose from, there's sure to be one that's just right for you! Break a leg!

SECTION 1
MONOLOGUES

1. Lions and Tigers and Mothers!

(Girl)

1   I can't believe my mom is making me take this stupid
2 role! I tried out for the witch, not Dorothy! Now, I have to
3 wear pigtails, for crying out loud. *(Stomps foot.)* There's no
4 way I'm wearing bobby socks and a blue-checkered dress.
5 It looks like a tablecloth. What idiotic director would look at
6 me and think "Dorothy"? Can't anyone see that I'm more of
7 a gothic black-dresser like the *witch*? Talk about mis-
8 casting!
9   I'll never be able to show my face in school again. I
10 wanted evil. Now I'm supposed to spout out ridiculous
11 songs about rainbows and birds and skip around like a
12 kindergartener. And if that's not bad enough, I've got to do
13 it with a scarecrow, a lion, and a man made out of tin! How
14 did this story ever last this long?
15   My costars are a bunch of *munchkins*, which means I've
16 got to spend rehearsals with a bunch of little kids from
17 elementary school trying to look and act like pint-sized
18 adults! It's ridiculous! I would've never signed up for
19 community theatre if I knew it was going to be like this. I
20 might as well have joined a kiddie show. Nobody's ever
21 going to take me seriously now.
22   This was supposed to help me grow — as an actress.
23 Well, this lame part couldn't grow a serious plot. I mean,
24 come on, *water* kills the witch? Do people really buy that
25 lame story line? I might as well kiss the witch to death.
26 We're the new generation. No one in their right mind wants
27 to see a play about water-melting-hocus-pocus-junk. I just
28 hope no one from school comes to see this thing! Or worse,

1   the high school drama director! I wouldn't want her type-
2   casting me for future plays as a goody-two-shoes character!
3   My whole acting career will be ruined!

2. I'd Like to "Poke Her Hontas!"

(Girl)

1   What a crock! Pocahontas gets a full-fledged, animated
2 movie with cute little animals and a talking tree and I get a
3 stupid coin? A filthy germ-ridden shove-it-in-your-drawer-
4 and-forget-about-it coin? What is everyone thinking? What
5 kind of heroine is she? I just don't understand what makes
6 that squaw so great.

7   She's not half the woman I am!

8   Who was kidnapped at age eleven? *Me.*

9   Who got married at the young age of fifteen? *Me.*

10   Who risked her life to save Lewis and Clark's journals
11 when their boat capsized? *Me!*

12   Me, me, *me!* Sacagawea! I'm the one everyone should be
13 talking about. I'm the one who should be the star of the
14 movies. I'm the one who little girls should be dressing up
15 like on Halloween. I'm the one whose life is worthy of a big-
16 screen movie! And songs to go with it! And merchandise:
17 T-shirts, dolls, stuffed animals. *Me!*

18   She wasn't anything but a long-haired, long-legged
19 attention stealer! Batting her dark lashes at every pale-
20 faced guy who came ashore. She wasn't interested in
21 peacemaking; she was interested in looking for a husband!
22 Is that the kind of woman you want your kids looking up to?
23 I don't think so!

24   How come I'm the only one who sees her for the gold
25 digger she really is! A movie? Get real! Maybe that talking
26 tree needs to whop someone upside the head! I'm tired of
27 playing second fiddle to that phony!

3. I'm Not a Blonde
(Girl)

1   I have three words for you: *I'm not blonde.* *(Pause)* **OK.**
2 **Wait a minute. That's four words. So, OK, like, I have four**
3 **words for you:** *I'm not blonde.* *(Pause)* **OK. Now wait ... does**
4 **a contraction count as one word or two? 'Cause it's like two**
5 **words in one, isn't it? But then when it has that little**
6 **comma thing then it's like one word, right? 'Cause it doesn't**
7 **have any space or anything ...** *(Counts.)*
8   **So then I really** *do* **have three words for you.** *I'm not a*
9 *blonde.* *(Counts while saying this and ends up with four*
10 *fingers.)* **Now, wait a minute. How did that happen?** *(Looks*
11 *confused, then sheepish.)* **Oh, duh, I added an "a" didn't I?**
12 *(Pause)* **But does that really count? 'Cause it's like one of**
13 **those non-words, isn't it? I mean, like, they don't even**
14 **capitalize it, do they? So maybe I shouldn't count it either.**
15   **So,** *(Counts again) I am not blonde. (Ends up with four*
16 *again.)* **Now hold on just a second. I** *know* **I only had three**
17 **words for you! It's like my words just keep multiplying or**
18 **something. This is really weird. I wonder what will happen if**
19 **I say it again.** *I am not a blonde. (Counts to five.)* **There! Did**
20 **you see that! Five words! I had four and now I've got five!**
21 **Omigosh. This is, like, amazing!**
22   **I'm like a human typewriter spitting out words. If I keep**
23 **talking, I bet a whole paragraph will come out!**

4. Bored Secret Agent
(Guy or girl)

1   " ... this message will self-destruct." Big deal! After
2   getting a lame assignment like this, *I'd* like to self-destruct!
3   I might as well work for the CIA ... or the army! My seven-
4   year-old niece could figure out where this guy's hiding!

5   He's practically walking around with a bull's-eye on his
6   head — hey, like that commercial where everyone's thinking
7   about that really juicy burger and so the restaurant logo is
8   hanging over their head. It's *that* obvious! Do they think I'm
9   losing it? Don't they trust me with the real stuff any more?
10   Do they think I've gone soft? 'Cause I'll show them soft!
11   Does a man with guns like these *(Holds up arms)* look soft
12   to you?

13   Where's my missile launcher? Or weapons of mass
14   destruction? Where are the challenging missions? I could do
15   *this* job with a slingshot and a rock! In fact, I may do that
16   just so I can have some fun!

17   Maybe it's time to get out of this business. Take my
18   talents elsewhere ...

19   But where? What could I possibly do? An ex-spy doesn't
20   have a lot of things to put on a resume, you know. I'd end
21   up working for some lame building security company
22   watching people make out on the elevator. Or at the mall
23   watching giggling girls try to shoplift nail polish or makeup.
24   There'd be no gun pulling or exciting chases! No midnight
25   rendezvous or secret messages to decode. Truth is, I
26   probably wouldn't even have handcuffs.

27   Aw, heck. I guess even a lame mission is better than
28   that!

5. Not a Football Fan
(Guy)

1   My school is completely fanatical about football. It's
2 completely normal to see kids with colored hair, painted
3 faces, and homemade T-shirts with the star quarterback's
4 name painted on them. And that's not even on game day.
5 It's completely ridiculous. This is only a middle school
6 football team! Not the NFL! Heck, it's not even high school!
7   But that's all anyone will talk about. It's not that I'm
8 anti-football. Really. If people want to get excited about
9 watching a bunch of boys gang up on each other, roll around
10 in the mud, and toss a stupid ball around, who I am to diss
11 it? I mean, it's *obviously* a sport requiring *extreme*
12 intelligence, so why *shouldn't* our school — our place of
13 *academic achievement* — completely endorse the football
14 frenzy? *(Very sarcastically)* Why shouldn't *everything* revolve
15 around that *one* sport, letting all other sports feel like the
16 stepchildren they are? It makes perfect sense doesn't it,
17 that the football jocks should be the most revered guys
18 around school? I mean, come on, they know how to ...
19 tackle ... and maybe even catch the ball sometimes!
20 Obviously life skills that will take them far in this world.
21   Why bother paying any attention to the future leaders of
22 the world? Possibly someone from the Academic Team,
23 Chess Club, or Math League? Maybe even someone from —
24 gasp! — you got it — *band!* Push those nerds aside, people!
25 We've got muscle walking down our halls! These guys are
26 going to put our town on the map one day! Show the world
27 what we're really made of!
28   OK. I lied. Maybe I am a *little* anti-football.

6. The Forgotten Principal
(Girl or guy)

1   You try and you try and then you try some more. You
2 work your little fingers to the bone, spend more hours in
3 your office than you do at home, and what does it get you?
4   Nothing! Absolutely nothing! Not a thank you. Not a
5 hand-drawn picture or a T-shirt with hand prints. Not even
6 a stinking bruised apple. Nothing. The teachers get it all. No
7 one ever thinks to get me anything. I'm just the mean old
8 principal.
9   Well, I'm just the one who keeps the school running!
10 Pays the bills. Does the paperwork. Makes sure there's food
11 for their little bellies!
12   But does anyone stop and think about that? Oh, no!
13 They must think this school just runs itself. That these kids
14 are good all on their own! Not a single parent, teacher, or
15 kid ever takes the time to say hello to me. Not even a casual
16 nod my way!
17   They're too busy flapping their jaws! Spreading
18 ridiculous rumors about me like I'm some kind of monster!
19 You should've heard the one last week — that I actually
20 threw a kid across a lunchroom table! Can you imagine? Do
21 I look strong enough to do something like that?
22   The truth is, everyone's so busy flattering their kids'
23 teachers to get their kids A's that they could care less
24 about showing appreciation for what I do! Well, you just
25 wait! The next kid I see, I'm giving a detention!

7. Envious Mermaid

(Girl)

1   These flippin' fins are getting on my nerves! Oh sure,
2 they're great for swimming, but other than that, what good
3 are they?

4   I see the people on the beach. The way their legs are
5 stretched out, soaking up the sun. Nice and dry. Not all
6 water-wrinkly like me! I haven't been totally dry a day in my
7 entire life! How I would love to feel the sand beneath my
8 toes. Feel the crunch of broken seashells beneath my feet.
9 But what do I get? Water, water, and more water! Quite
10 frankly, I think I'm getting seasick!

11   I mean, look at me: part fish, part girl. Who ever heard
12 of such a thing? It's like I don't belong in either world! What
13 kind of life is that? Never feeling like you belong? I just want
14 to live a normal life — on land — like everyone else!

15   *(Pauses and becomes more melancholy.)* **Of course, I would**
16 miss it ... the sea. Riding the crest of a wave. Swimming
17 alongside a school of dolphins. Discovering hidden caves
18 and sunken ships.

19   And my family. I'm pretty sure *they've* never dreamt of
20 living on the land. They're perfectly happy being half and
21 half. I'd never see them again. That'd be hard. I'd really miss
22 my sisters ... well, most of them anyway.

23   Oh, the land seems so inviting. So different ...

24   If only I could feel the sand between my toes!

8. Not a Nerd Lover
(Girl)

1   Sometimes I think I *would* be better off with that geeky
2 little nerd in band class. I mean, he practically adores the
3 ground I walk on. Every day ... notes in my locker, gifts on
4 my desk. But ewwww! He plays the flute! How pathetic is
5 that? He'll probably live with his mother until he's in his
6 thirties!

7   I want a real man. A take-charge kind of guy.
8 Determined. Someone who never gives up. But Todd, star
9 quarterback, won't even look twice at me! I've done
10 everything I can think of. Gone to every game. Made
11 homemade signs to cheer him on. I've even hung out with
12 his younger sister just so I could be near him. Last time I
13 was over at his house, I even brought dog treats for his dog!
14 Do you know what happened? That dirty mongrel licked me!
15 And I don't mean Todd either! I had to run home and
16 disinfect my face!

17   Then, when I heard Todd was trying out for track, I tried
18 out, too. You know, love your man, love his sports! But he
19 was so doggone slow there was no way I could let him beat
20 me. I would've had to crawl across the finish line to do that.
21 I figure that'll be our cute little story though. You know, how
22 I beat the big macho jock guy at track. One day, after he
23 comes to his senses and we're married and have grandkids,
24 he'll be like, "Remember when you used to beat me every
25 race? It's what made me fall in love with you, Tracy." It'll be
26 our special romantic story.

27   Well, it *would* be our romantic story if I could ever get
28 him to stop talking about that stupid little red-haired

1   cheerleader. The one who couldn't *find* the track, much less
2   beat him on it! He practically drools when he talks about
3   her.
4   I've tried playing that game, too. Acting like I adore the
5   nerd guy in band just to make Todd jealous. I don't think
6   he's even noticed. And I get stuck listening to flute boy
7   describe the challenges of playing a trill — whatever the
8   heck that is! Oh, who am I kidding, I could never go with a
9   guy like that!

9. This Can't be My Real Family
(Girl or guy)

1 There's really no other explanation. No logical reason for
2 how *I* could actually be *born* into a family like this. In fact,
3 it's absolutely impossible to believe that I could share the
4 same blood as anyone who lives in this house! So of course
5 I'm adopted. It's the only thing that makes sense.
6   I mean, look at them! My father is disgusting! Do you
7 know what he did last week? Ate a piece of pizza that was
8 almost a week old. That had been left on the counter the
9 whole time! That's right — no refrigeration! Can't you get
10 botulism from something like that?
11   You want to know *why* he ate it? Because he was too
12 lazy to fix himself something for dinner. He'd rather eat
13 stale, gross food than take out a pan and cook something.
14 He thinks we all live to serve him, and if we're not around,
15 he just sits and waits for us.
16   My brother isn't any better. He's constantly doing stupid
17 things. He has no fear of getting in trouble. He's been
18 suspended more times than I've made the honor roll, and
19 believe me, that's saying a lot! He's going to end up in
20 prison before he even gets out of elementary school.
21   My younger sister isn't so bad. It's hard to tell how she's
22 going to turn out, though. I suspect she's going to be
23 somewhat of an idiot. All she does is suck her pacifier. And
24 she's five years old! She actually packs her "pacy" in her
25 backpack. There's something seriously wrong with that, you
26 know?
27   Mom is probably the best of the bunch, but she's
28 obviously no genius. Why would she stay with such a loser,

1   much less marry him in the first place! Where were her
2   standards? Her expectations? Did she really want to be
3   saddled with a man who eats crumbs out of his belly button?
4   I guess since she didn't get married until she was thirty, she
5   was afraid to be too picky. But come on, "**Mom**" *(Air quotes*
6   *around Mom)*, I *know* you could've done better than this!

10. Why Grow Up?
(Guy)

1   I don't ever want to be a grown-up. I don't. I mean, look
2 at them! Their faces are all sour and stern and old looking!
3 Why would I ever want to be one of them? They walk around
4 like robot-people. No expression. No smile. No life! It's like
5 they're half-dead already! What normal teen would ever
6 want to become one of those? No time for hanging out with
7 your friends, listening to music, going skateboarding! All
8 work and no play! What kind of life is that, I ask you?

9   The highlight of their day is watching boring news shows
10 or reading the newspaper! The newspaper! For real fun, they
11 read the obituaries and look for people they know. Now,
12 that's excitement, isn't it? Checking to see how everyone
13 died!

14   What smart guy would ever want to be a man? I say
15 avoid the whole working-yourself-to-death thing for as long
16 as possible. My parents have been after me since I turned
17 twelve to get a job. Work a paper route. Mow lawns. I say,
18 "What's the rush?" I've got my whole life in front of me.

19   I think they just can't wait for me to be as miserable as
20 they are! Working that whole eight-to-five thing. That's
21 crazy! Who wants to spend those kind of hours at work?
22 When would I sleep? Watch TV? Call my friends?

23   Well, they can ask all they want, but I'm not budging.
24 What are they going to do, kick me out? Ha! Maybe they
25 could if they weren't working all the time!

11. Worst Best Friend Ever
(Guy)

1   Take my advice. Never, ever be best friends with the
2 hottest guy in school. Every day it's *Brian this* and *Brian*
3 *that*. And "Hey, have you seen Brian?" Like I'm supposed to
4 keep track of him twenty-four-seven. I'm so sick of
5 everything being all about him! Hello?! What about me? I
6 may not be the school stud, but I'm definitely not chopped
7 liver. I feel like the guy's shadow.
8   It didn't used to be this way. In fact, in sixth grade, no
9 one even paid attention to Brian. He was overweight, wore
10 glasses, and was shorter than half the girls in class. I had
11 more girlfriends that year than he did. Actually, I don't even
12 remember Brian having a girlfriend at all. No one would go
13 out with him!
14   But something happened over the summer. He shot up,
15 like, a couple of feet! His zits are almost entirely gone, and
16 the guy has seriously slimmed down and bulked up in all the
17 right places. And he got some really cool blue contacts. All
18 of a sudden, he's morphed into the most popular guy in
19 school. And of course, he suddenly discovered basketball
20 and, wouldn't you know, the guy can play. Well enough to be
21 a starter his first year on the team. If I wasn't his friend, I
22 could easily hate him. *(Pause)* To be totally honest, I would
23 hate him if he wasn't so nice. And if it weren't for the fact
24 that we've been friends since we were altar boys at church.
25   And — I'm not going to lie — there are some fringe
26 benefits to the position. Like when he can't decide which of
27 two girls to take to the monthly school dance, so he throws
28 one my way. Pity dates, I know, but hey, sometimes you've
29 got to take what you can get. Maybe one day I'll morph into
30 Mr. Stud Man.

12. Abandoned

(Guy or girl)

1   *(Angry)* **So I'm just supposed to throw open my arms**
2 **and act like nothing happened? Forget all these years where**
3 **Mr. CEO was too busy to even notice me? He was so intent**
4 **on staying head honcho that he barely even acknowledged**
5 **that he had a kid. Best I ever got was a nod in my direction**
6 **whenever he walked by. And then after he left Mom, I was**
7 **lucky if I ever heard from him. Not even birthday cards. Now**
8 **Mom dies and suddenly he wants back in my life?**

9   **Well, what if I don't want *him* back? I might as well live**
10 **with strangers. I don't even *know* him. Why did they even**
11 **contact him? There are certainly other people I could live**
12 **with. People who actually know and love me. I don't need**
13 **him acting like my father now.**

14   **I guess I should be grateful that he even came back. He**
15 **could've gone off, *as usual*, and not even bothered. But**
16 **grateful isn't even close to how I feel.**

17   **Why couldn't he have been the one who died? Why did it**
18 **have to be my mom? What did she ever do to deserve that?**
19 **She's the one that was always there for me. Putting on the**
20 **Band-aids. Coming to my games. Helping me with**
21 **homework. Where was he during all that? Was running a**
22 **company more important than caring for me?**

23   **He made his choice, and now I'm making mine. I haven't**
24 **had a real father since the day I was born. I don't need one**
25 **now. I'd rather live with other relatives, or friends. Heck, I'd**
26 **rather go to foster care.**

13. Scary Movie Blonde

(Girl)

1   OK. So you know the dumb blonde in the horror movies
2 that you're always screaming things at? Like — *don't go in*
3 *there! What are you doing? Are you out of your mind? Oh,*
4 *come on! Who goes out in the dark when they hear a noise?*
5 *No one!*

6   Well, that's me. The dumb blonde. I didn't think it was.
7 Really. I've yelled at the same stupid people you have and
8 then — last night — it happened! I turned into one of those
9 brain-dead, "hello? Is-someone-there?" people! I didn't even
10 realize it at first.

11   See, I got home from practice last night and the house
12 was totally dark. Not a car in the driveway. No big deal.
13 Mom and Dad often come home after me. They're both
14 classic workaholics. I wave my friend's mother on so that
15 she won't have to wait for me to dig through my bag and
16 find my key.

17   Then I get to the door — open. Not just unlocked, but
18 part of the way open! Now here's where the scary music
19 should've started — you know, clued me in that maybe
20 something was wrong. But did it? No. Complete and utter
21 silence.

22   So what do I do? Yell. Of course, because that's what
23 every idiot blonde does. "Hello? Anyone there?" Like all axe
24 murderers are polite enough to answer back when you yell
25 for them.

26   No answer. Duh. So that means it's safe, right? 'Cause
27 no one answered. I hurry up and go in and lock the door
28 behind me because I want to make *sure* that I lock myself

1   *in* with the psycho killer, right? I mean, that's what the
2   dumb screaming blonde always does.
3   I turn on every light in the house as I go through it —
4   searching every closet and hiding spot I know of. Well,
5   except the basement — it's dark and scary down there and
6   I'm not *that* blonde. And it makes perfect sense that no axe
7   murderer would possibly want to hide down there, right?!
8   I'm on the last round through the house when there is a
9   huge crash outside. So what do I do? Run to the door, open
10 it, and yell, "Hello? Is someone out there?" I rush outside.
11 But don't worry — I leave the door *wide open* so that I can
12 run back in! Yes, yet another stupid blonde move! But thank
13 goodness I got back in safe and sound, no axe murderer
14 lying in wait! Luckily my parents showed up a few hours
15 later — their daughter all in one piece and not hacked up
16 and scattered around the house!
17   Tomorrow, I'm dying my hair red!

14. A Ride to Remember

(Guy or girl)

1   I cannot *wait* to *get my license.* You have *no* idea. I know
2 it's still three years away, but it's all I can think of! It's not
3 just your average turning-sixteen, can't-wait-to-drive-and-
4 have-a-little-independence syndrome. This is a life and
5 death situation. Seriously — if I don't get me and my friends
6 out of my mother's car, I'm going to grab the steering wheel
7 and crash us all into the nearest tree!

8   You think I'm kidding? Hop in for a spin. It's not the
9 constant slamming of the brakes, or the incessant blinker
10 that she never turns off, or even the occasional grazing of
11 the curb — oh no! Those I can live with. Those are normal,
12 get-under-your-skin-but-deal-with-it things that any kid can
13 live with. This is so much worse.

14   It's the *singing.* The top-of-your-lungs, screeching-like-
15 an-owl, can't-hit-a-note singing from the moment the engine
16 starts. She thinks she's being cool because she listens to
17 the same music that I do — which, OK — could be cool *if*
18 she'd keep her mouth shut!

19   She doesn't even know the words! Just makes them up
20 as she goes. Do you think a teeny little thing like not
21 knowing the words would stop her? Of course not! They
22 don't even make sense! The other day — I swear this is
23 true, I am not making this up — how could anyone make
24 something like this up — she sang about a *salad bar!* Who
25 in their right mind sings about a salad bar? How could she
26 possibly think the words in a rap song would be about a
27 stupid salad bar?!

28   It's so humiliating. I'm seriously considering getting a

1   bike and riding it everywhere! At least until I get my own car

2   and then if Mom rides with me — the radio stays *off!* *(Slaps*

3   *head.)* Oh, no! Then she'd be singing a cappella!

15. Ticked-Off Park Character
(Guy)

1   I am so sick of wearing this stupid costume. I can't wait
2 for summer to be over. Even school is better than this! I
3 think I've lost ten pounds in sweat this summer wearing this
4 stupid getup. It must be a thousand degrees in here.

5   Every day, all day long, it's the same thing. Smiles.
6 Hugs. Wave until your arm's sore. Kids sitting on my lap ...
7 speaking of which — parents, get a clue! You are too big —
8 let me make this perfectly clear — too *fat* to sit on my lap!
9 See this? For kids only. I do *not* think it's cute when you
10 want your picture taken, too. I do *not* think it's cute when
11 you kiss and hug me. In fact, it makes me want to call the
12 cops — you stupid pervs! You don't go around sitting on
13 Santa's lap, do you? The Easter Bunny? Well, don't sit on
14 me!

15   To top things off, I gotta sign stupid little autograph
16 books all day like I'm some kind of celebrity or something.
17 I can barely hold the pen in my paw. But do they care? No.
18 They act like they're going to have a stroke if they don't get
19 my signature! The parents are the worst — shoving their
20 kids through the crowd like I'm handing out money or
21 something. What are they going to do — sell their autograph
22 books on the web? Priceless autograph books full of *fake*
23 autographs from *fake* people! Now that's going to bring in
24 some money!

25   I don't even look real. I mean, come on, people. My eyes
26 are sewn on. I've got a zipper up my back and an air hole
27 for a mouth! Do these stupid kids really think I look like the
28 animated version they've seen on television? It stinks that

1   this is the only place around that they're desperate enough
2   to hire thirteen-year-olds! I'm sweating to death in this suit.
3   Next year I'm signing up to be that dude from *The Jungle*
4   *Book* — he's practically naked!

16. Prepaid? Are You Kidding Me?

(Girl)

1   My parents are being so ridiculous! How can they expect
2   me to use this thing? Look at it! It's an antique! They
3   haven't made cell phones this big since ... I don't know ...
4   since cavemen used them, I guess! I can't even fit the thing
5   in my pocket. And prepaid? Are they kidding me? Do they
6   have any idea how expensive that's going to be? How is that
7   teaching me responsibility? Making me pay outrageous
8   amounts of money just to be able to text my friends!

9   Why can't I be on *their* plan? They have *unlimited*
10   texting, and they don't even know how to use it! My mother
11   has had a flashing envelope on her phone for two months
12   now. When I try to show her how to read it, she just glazes
13   over like I'm speaking another language and then says
14   stupid things like, "Well, nobody uses that anyway. Why
15   would they text me when they can just call me?"

16   Hello?! Nobody calls any more! What century is she
17   living in? I have friends who text over three thousand
18   messages a month! A month! Do my completely clueless
19   parents have *any* idea how much that would cost me? Let's
20   see, three thousand times twenty-five cents apiece ... that's
21   ... well ... I'm not good at math, but I know that's a whole
22   lot of money!

23   I might as well not have a phone if I have to have this
24   one! I'm too embarrassed to use it in public! It looks like a
25   walkie-talkie instead of a phone. And it doesn't even have a
26   camera! I didn't know they still *made* phones without
27   cameras! How am I supposed to send my friends pictures?
28   Oh, this is so lame. They can just have it back. Until they
29   put me on a real phone plan, I don't even want a cell phone!

17. Limo Spells Lame-o For Me!
(Girl)

1   This just can't be happening to me. It can't! The same
2 day I give out my birthday invitations to all my friends, this
3 has to happen! It's completely unfair. And, might I say, just
4 a little bit over the top. Who in their right mind has a school
5 limo pick up for a thirteenth birthday party? *(Pause)* Well,
6 someone with *totally cool* and *awesome* parents, that's who!
7 Do you know how amazing it'll be waving at everyone as they
8 head for the busses and *we* slip into a limo? We'll feel like
9 celebrities! It'll probably be the best night of our lives!

10   How can I possibly follow a fantastic night like that?
11 Anything I do for my birthday is going to be pathetic. My
12 friends are going to laugh when they read my invitation now.
13 Pizza and PJs and a lame-o sleepover. *In my basement!*
14 That doesn't even have heat! How's that for giving your
15 friends the royal treatment? My mom might as well break
16 out the milk and cookies now. It'll feel like a kindergarten
17 party! I'm completely humiliated.

18   Why did this have to happen to me? Why couldn't Ashley
19 have been born after me — like six months or so! Then I
20 could've gone first. I could've followed Shelly's party — she
21 didn't even have anyone spend the night! We just hung out
22 at her house and basically gave her gifts. Great for her.
23 Boring for us.

24   But what am I going to do now? I can't expect the same
25 friends who are going out in style for Ashley's party one
26 week to ride the *bus* to my house the next! I might as well
27 take back my invitations. No one's going to show up
28 anyway. Well, there's one good thing about it all: At least I
29 won't have to clean the basement now!

18. Candy Bars for Sale
(Guy)

1   I think I've totally missed the concept of fundraising. I'm
2   supposed to sell things to *other* people to earn money for
3   the class trip — not buy the stupid things myself! I'm down
4   fifteen bucks already! Whoever came up with the idea of
5   selling candy bars was crazy! How can they expect me —
6   how can they expect *any* teenage guy — to pack around this
7   box of goodies all day and *not* eat any! It's pure torture.

8   Even if I *do* want to sell them and not eat them, no one
9   wants to buy one from me. Not when all the cute
10 cheerleaders are selling them, too. Let's see ... buy from the
11 geek in math class or the hot cheerleader with the cute little
12 bow in her hair? I haven't got a chance. Even the girls buy
13 from the cheerleaders because they want to be noticed by
14 them. They all wish they can fit into the popular crowd and
15 maybe — just maybe if they're really lucky and they buy
16 enough candy bars — they'll get a bow in their hair, too!

17 It's pathetic. I can't even get the teachers to buy from
18 me. Everyone's on a diet! Duh! It's January. *Everyone* in the
19 *entire world* starts a diet at the first of the year. All the
20 would-be skinny people see me coming and run the other
21 way. I can't even unload one of these four hundred and fifty-
22 calorie bars on people who actually are skinny because even
23 though they aren't worried about weight — they're worried
24 about being healthy! Of course they are! That's New Year's
25 resolution number two! Eat healthier!

26 The way I see it, I've got two choices. Forget the
27 fundraising and just pay for the trip, or eat all the candy
28 bars I want to earn my fifty cents on the dollar to pay for the

1   trip. It'll take me longer, but hey, if I'm going to pay anyway,

2   I might as well get something for it!

19. Purse Party

(Girl)

1   This is getting ridiculous! It's bad enough getting invited
2 to a gazillion people's birthdays every year and having to
3 buy them presents, but now I'm expected to go to my
4 friends' houses and buy things *from them*? This kind of
5 thing is for old ladies or people with money! Where am I
6 supposed to get the cash to buy a forty-dollar — or more —
7 purse? And don't forget the matching wallet! I won't be able
8 to leave without getting one of those!

9   Next my friends will be inviting me to buy dishes, or
10 makeup, or jewelry. Just so *they* can get free stuff and I can
11 be broke! I don't even get an allowance. But if I did, I still
12 wouldn't be buying stuff like that! That's what my parents
13 are for! *My* money is for fun stuff like candy, and CDs, and
14 things that I want!

15   I know what's going to happen, though. I'm going to go
16 — it's not like I have a choice, she's my *best* friend! — and
17 I'll feel all guilty and order something. Something I cannot
18 afford. And then I'll have to do all these extra chores around
19 the house to earn money, just to buy a stupid purse that I
20 didn't *want* or *need* in the first place!

21   This *so* stinks! Who cares about fake designer purses
22 anyway? The ones I've seen look like something my
23 grandma would carry! And even if I do see a cute one, I'd
24 rather buy it at the store with my mom's money where it'll
25 probably be half the price.

26   Well, I'm just going to have to find a way out. Get sick.
27 Say my cat ran away. Too much homework. Something.
28 Anything! I will not cave in to the purse frenzy that has
29 taken over my school!

20. Smelly Pants
(Guy)

1   There are certainly valid reasons for a guy to be called
2   "Smelly Pants." Maybe even admirable ones if you're into
3   the whole burping, farting, and scratching like a guy thing.
4   I'm not. And I did *not* earn the nickname "Smelly Pants" for
5   the usual reasons.

6   It all happened in third grade, and here I am in middle
7   school and I still can't shake it off. Let me just say that I
8   am a very picky eater. Always have been. I would sit for
9   hours at the table with food sitting in front of me and never
10   touch it. Many nights my parents sent me to bed hungry
11   because I wouldn't eat what Mom had fixed. What can I say?
12   I like what I like and I despise what I don't like. Makes me
13   gag.

14   So one night Mom gets the brilliant idea to make corned
15   beef and cabbage. Two nasty things alone ... even nastier
16   when combined. The smell of the cabbage cooking made me
17   want to vomit. Luckily she invited my aunt and uncle and
18   their kids over to eat with us, which meant an "adult" table
19   in the kitchen and a "kid" table in the dining room.

20   I wasn't the *only* one wanting to gag that night. In fact,
21   I'm pretty sure that if my cousins had known what Mom was
22   serving they would've faked an illness so as not to come!

23   We devised a plan. We could choke down the meat; it
24   was the least disgusting of the two. But the cabbage was a
25   no-go. Unfortunately, I was the only one at the table with
26   pockets. Everyone passed me their plates and I stuffed the
27   cabbage in both my pockets. Cabbage juice trickled down
28   my legs. I told Mom I was going out to play and then I

1 dumped the cabbage in the ditch.

2   Later that night, when I was in bed, I figured I'd been
3 pretty smart. Mom didn't know any differently, and I didn't
4 have to eat the cabbage.

5   I should've known that Mom was much smarter than me.
6 When my pants came back in the laundry basket the next
7 week, they were distinctively smelly. Like maybe Mom had
8 forgotten to actually *wash* them. They reeked of cabbage.

9   Mom laid them on my bed for me to wear. What could I
10 do? Admit what I'd done, or wear them to school anyway?
11 Of course I decided to wear them. If I didn't, I knew I was
12 looking at cooked cabbage for at least a week of meals!

13   It didn't take long for the smell to waft through the bus.
14 Pretty soon every window was open and every nose was
15 being plugged. And that's why — to this day — I'm still
16 called "Smelly Pants."

21. Snobbish Older Sister
(Guy)

1   My sister is such a snob. She thinks that just because
2 she's in *high school*, she's too good to drive me to school.
3 She can't stand the thought of her friends seeing her driving
4 a lowly middle-schooler around like a chauffeur. The few
5 times my mom has forced her to take me, she makes me
6 ride in the back and duck down whenever we pass a car that
7 *might* be driven by someone she knows. And she drops me
8 off as far from where I need to go as humanly possible.
9 She'll say, "This is as good as it gets, bro. Now get out."
10 Like actually turning into the parking lot of the school would
11 be too much trouble for her!

12   I thought having a sister who could drive would be cool.
13 That she'd take me all sorts of places without Mom and Dad
14 tagging along. We'd be free! Maybe even a little wild and crazy!

15   Ha! Not even close. She got her license two months ago,
16 and I've ridden in the car with her alone three times. *(Holds*
17 *up fingers.)* That's right, folks! Count 'em! *Three times!* What
18 happened to, "You'll be driving your brother to school," or
19 "I'll need you to take Brian to football practices
20 sometimes." What happened to that, I ask you? I've had to
21 walk to practice twice this week! While she sat at home
22 doing nothing! She could've driven me. But no! Said she
23 needed to save gas. *Save gas!* We live less than a mile from
24 the school! How much gas could that take? Even in the
25 super-tank she drives?

26   You know what? I don't even care any more. Truth is, I'd
27 rather walk than ride in that death trap with her! She should
28 be embarrassed by her car, not me! The muffler has a hole
29 in it that's bigger than her fat snobbish head!

22. Copycat Kids
(Girl)

1   Every summer I volunteer to work at Vacation Bible
2 School. It's pretty fun, and I get to be the boss of about
3 twenty little first graders. It's better than baby duty where
4 you have to change diapers and get puked on. Every other
5 year I've had to be the helper for the adult. This year,
6 though, either they were desperate, or they've grown to
7 trust me because they put me in charge of the whole group.
8 I actually had someone helping me! It was awesome. Those
9 kids followed me around the place like a bunch of little
10 ducklings. Everything I did, they did. Like a continuous
11 game of copycat.

12   It was cute at first. Like twenty little mini-mes. Quite a
13 compliment, really, that they wanted to be so much like me.
14 But then the worst possible thing that could ever happen
15 happened! I was pouring the red Kool-aid for their snack. I
16 had on my favorite white shirt. The pitcher slipped from my
17 hands ... and a bad word slipped from my mouth.

18   All of their little faces registered complete shock. Which
19 actually is better than what happened next. See, all of my
20 little mini-mes started saying the bad word — over and over
21 — like a chant! I don't know if they knew what it was or not,
22 but they knew from my face that it wasn't something I
23 wanted them to say! Which just made them say it more.
24 The more I hushed them, the louder they got until they were
25 practically screaming the bad word at the tops of their
26 lungs. Even the cute little girl in pigtails who never spoke a
27 single word all week was screaming it out.

28   It didn't take long for the Children's Director to find out.

1   Probably had twenty sets of parents calling her all night.
2   She met me at the door the next night. Now I'm a helper in
3   the nursery. With the babies who can't talk. *(Shrugs.)* I don't
4   really blame her ... but I sure will miss all those little mini-
5   mes!

23. Used Clothes?
Are You Kidding Me?
(Girl)

1   I was completely misled! Bought into the commercial
2 that promised name-brand clothes for *way less* than
3 department stores! Thought I was going to save my mother
4 a couple of bucks. Make her happy and get me more
5 clothes. But I should have known! We drive up and the store
6 is not even in a mall! It's in a shopping center. An *old*, run-
7 down shopping center! That was the first clue.

8   Second clue: a woman walking *in* to the store with a
9 garbage bag. Now, I may not be the smartest kid in school,
10 but I knew right away that something was up with that!

11   "Is this a used clothing store?" I asked my mom with
12 obvious disgust. She was beaming ear to ear like we'd just
13 found a million dollars or something.

14   "Well, I'm not going in there!" I tell her because I am
15 literally dying at the thought that someone might actually
16 *see* me walking into a place like that. Ohmigosh! They would
17 think that we were poor ... or just completely *gross!*

18   But Mom won't back down. "Oh, no," she says. "You
19 begged me to bring you here, and now we're here!"

20   "I was tricked. The ad didn't say it was cheap because
21 someone else had worn it! That's disgusting!"

22   My mother had the audacity to roll her eyes at me!
23 "Yeah. Because so many gross and disgusting people can
24 afford those name brand clothes in the first place. Quit
25 being a snob and come on."

26   She made me stay in there for over an hour. My skin felt
27 like it was crawling at first, but eventually I forgot where I
28 was. I found some great shirts that were practically new!

1   And they were cheap, too. I got three for less than the price
2   of one at the mall.

3   "We're definitely washing them before I wear them," I
4   told my mom as we walked to the car.

5   "Of course," she said.

6   "And you can *never* tell *anyone* we were here!" I made
7   her promise. Told her I might even come back if she
8   promised not to tell. She did, and we've been back two
9   times since then. Good news is that with the money we've
10 saved, Mom let me buy a new hair straightener! I hate to
11 admit it, but maybe used clothes aren't so bad after all.

24. Can't Smile Without Tooth
(Guy)

1   When I was in fifth grade my dad got me a mini bike. We
2 live on a farm, so I had plenty of space to ride. And I did.
3 Every day. Up and down the fence line and in between the
4 cornrows. That was the first week.
5   The second week I became more daring. I mounded up
6 dirt and made jumps, and when they weren't high enough,
7 I took some of Dad's lumber from the barn and made
8 ramps. It was the greatest feeling to fly through the air. And
9 I was pretty good at it, too. Of course I began envisioning a
10 lifetime of motorcycle championships and hot girls in
11 skimpy clothes hanging all over me.
12   My mom was not so crazy about the bike. She made me
13 wear all sorts of gear and nagged me constantly about being
14 safe. But what does safe mean to a ten-year-old boy? The
15 ramps got higher and higher until one day I sailed right into
16 a tree. The helmet probably saved my life — my face wasn't
17 so lucky. I had a ton of scratches and cuts — two that
18 needed stitches. But the worst part was, a branch knocked
19 out one of my front teeth! Even that wasn't so bad once I
20 got a fake one, though. And I had a great story to tell. I was
21 like the Evel Knievel of the fifth grade. Probably why I got
22 my first kiss that year.
23   And why I always have a girlfriend now in middle school.
24 A reputation like that follows you a long time! Which is why
25 I know that after last night, I will never have a date again!
26   See, last night I thought Hannah and I would do
27 something different. We always go to the movies or out to
28 eat. We've got this new bowling alley in town, and it seemed

1   like a good idea. Our parents were more than happy to drop
2   us off there. It was fun, too. At first. I threw a couple of
3   strikes — totally by luck — so I was feeling pretty good.
4   Then they turned on the fog. And the regular lighting
5   switched to black lights. I didn't think anything about it. So
6   there I was grinning like an idiot at Hannah when she busts
7   up laughing. I'm like, "What? What's so funny?" But every
8   time I open my mouth, she laughs even harder and hands
9   me a mirror.

10   I always knew my fake tooth was a slightly different
11 color and texture than my real ones. But come on — a tooth
12 that actually glows? What sick dentist came up with such a
13 thing? How come no one warned me? In one short moment,
14 I went from being the tough motorcycle guy to the moron
15 with the neon tooth! How is that even fair?

25. Cats Rule and Dogs Drool
(Guy)

1   So I have this cat. He's really cool, too. He's like the dog
2 version of a cat. He follows me everywhere and even waits
3 at the door for me whenever I leave him. He's completely
4 loyal to me. He won't even think about sleeping with anyone
5 else in the house.

6   Apparently, though, a cat is not an acceptable pet for a
7 guy. Especially not for a macho football player. Ever since
8 the team found out I have a cat, they've been relentless.
9 They'll shout things like, "Trey misses his kitty cat," or
10 "Trey tackles like a girl. Maybe he needs a dog to rough him
11 up." Like I'm not a man without a dog. It's completely
12 ridiculous. My cat has more brains and personality than all
13 of their stupid dogs combined. Half of them don't even see
14 their dogs. They keep them caged up in a pen and only take
15 them out for hunting. What kind of a pet is that? Why even
16 have a dog if you're not going to hang out with it?

17   Tiger is like my best friend. He even talks to me. Not
18 people talk, of course — I'm not crazy. But every morning
19 he'll meow this little conversation with me, like he's really
20 trying to tell me something. Show me a dog that does that!

21   And he's a hunter, too. He's brought home more mice
22 and moles — and even snakes — than any stupid dog has.
23 Why is it that just because a cat is cute and fluffy it makes
24 the owner less manly? We like girls, and *they're* all cute and
25 cuddly! So I say what's wrong with being a cat lover? They
26 can call me anything they want — I'm keeping my kitty cat!
27 Cats rule and dogs drool!

26. Copycat Classmate
(Girl)

1   You know that game you played when you were little
2 where you would mimic everything the other person said?
3 Even your parents, and they'd get mad and be like, "Stop
4 repeating me." And you'd be like, "Stop repeating me." And
5 they'd say, "I mean it." And you'd say, "I mean it." And
6 then they'd say, "If you don't stop, you're going to get in
7 trouble." And yes, you, being young and dumb, would be
8 like, "If you don't stop, you're going to get in trouble." And
9 on and on it went until you got sent to your room or
10 grounded from TV? Well, that is my life right now!

11   See, there's this girl in school, and even though she
12 doesn't copy everything I say, she might as well! She does
13 absolutely *everything* I do. If I start parting my hair on the
14 left, she starts parting *her* hair on the left. If I start wearing
15 socks with my shoes, she starts wearing socks with *her*
16 shoes. If I wear blue eye shadow, *she* wears blue eye
17 shadow. You get the idea, right? She's like a mini-me, and
18 it's driving me completely crazy.

19   I've even tried tricking her. One day I'll say, "Oh, I hate
20 it when people tuck in their shirts." She'll agree and so the
21 next day I'll tuck in my shirt and by second hour, she'll have
22 hers tucked in, too. I don't think she knows how to be
23 anything else but a clone of me! It's almost scary. Like
24 she's a stalker or something.

25   My mom keeps saying that it's a compliment when
26 someone tries to act like you. Well, it sure doesn't *feel* like
27 a compliment. It's creepy! Doesn't this chick have a mind of
28 her own? I truly believe if I jumped off a cliff, that psycho

1 girl would follow me! But I've got a plan. From now on, I'm
2 wearing khakis and a button-down shirt. Every day! Let's
3 see how long mini-me wants to copy that!

27. Writing Scared

(Guy or girl)

1   OK. So if you were to write about a talking vegetable,
2   you wouldn't really believe that vegetables talked, right?
3   That would be insane! And if you were to write about
4   animals that wore clothes and lived in houses, you wouldn't
5   really expect to see a moving truck pull up and a couple of
6   bears get out, right?

7   So what is wrong with me? I am a writer. Started writing
8   the minute I could put a sentence together. I love it. But for
9   some reason when I write, weird things come to mind. Scary
10   things. Horrible things. The kind of stuff that would make
11   little kids sleep with their parents for the rest of their lives.
12   That's not so crazy, though, because lots of good writers
13   write about creepy, scary stuff. The bad thing is, even
14   though I *say* I don't believe the stuff I write, deep down, I
15   most certainly do! And that's why I can't sleep at night!

16   I've scared myself to the point where extreme paranoia
17   has set in. I process every noise. Every sound in the house
18   is analyzed and catalogued in my mind as to which type of
19   intruder has broken into my house. Serial killer? Axe
20   murderer? Alien? Yes. That's right. Alien. I'm talking bizarre
21   stuff!

22   And if I'm not worried about what's going to happen *to*
23   me, I'm worried about what's *wrong* with me! What kind of
24   sick person thinks of the things I do? How come I can even
25   dream up these horrible, dice 'em and slice 'em scenes that
26   I write about? What if there's something evil inside of me?
27   What if this is just the beginning? What if I'm not really
28   writing novels, but an action plan? How did Edgar Allen Poe
29   survive? I'm really scaring the you-know-what out of me!

28. What Was I Thinking?

(Guy)

1   So, it seemed like a good idea at the time. Something
2 unique. Something different. I mean, everyone paints the
3 walls, right? So why *not* paint something cool on the ceiling?
4   Well, I'll tell you why not! My neck is killing me! My
5 muscles are so sore and knotted; it'll take some intensive
6 physical therapy to work these kinks out. What was I
7 thinking? Why would anyone want to hold a paintbrush up
8 over their heads for hours at a time? I've tried other ways —
9 lying down on the scaffolding — but I still have to hold my
10 arm up! The paintbrush feels like it weighs a hundred
11 pounds! And I've dripped paint in my eyes so many times
12 that I think I'm crying in color!
13   Why couldn't I have been smart and picked the floor
14 instead? At least people would've seen it. Who is ever even
15 going to notice this thing way up here? And *their* necks will
16 get sore if they look at it too long. No one in their right mind
17 is going to go through all that just to look at a painting. My
18 arm muscles are so strained; the lines are starting to look
19 shaky! People will be talking about this horrible paint job for
20 centuries! But I can't stop now! I can't have half a ceiling
21 painted. My reputation is at stake. I'd never get another
22 paint job again.
23   Maybe I could try that hot new contemporary art stuff
24 I've been hearing about. I'll just throw some paint cans at
25 the ceiling and see what happens ... but, oh ... my
26 masterpiece ... I cannot degrade myself that way. Let me
27 just call a masseuse and I'll get back up on that ladder!

29. Watched Like a Hawk
(Guy)

1   If your dad is a surgeon, nobody expects you to operate
2   by default, right? And if your dad is a policeman, they sure
3   don't hand over a gun and tell you to serve and protect,
4   right? So why is it that just because my dad is a minister,
5   everyone expects me to act like one, too?
6   I'm sick of everyone in the church watching my every
7   move. They can't wait to whisper and gossip about me.
8   They expect me to be the perfect little angel. Well, I didn't
9   sign up for this! I am not the one standing up at the pulpit
10   preaching to everyone. I don't see anyone else's kid being
11   scrutinized the way I am. Because I could sure tell some
12   stories about the kids in youth group, let me tell you! Their
13   parents are church-goers — how come they get to act that
14   way and I can't even slip and say a bad word without it
15   being printed in the bulletin!
16   And now, I *finally* have a girl brave enough to date me
17   — that's right! *Brave* enough! It's like having the paparazzi
18   watching your every move. Who wants to put up with that?
19   But she does, and she's great about it. And I can't even
20   hold her hand or put my arm around her because I have to
21   be held to a higher standard! Well, I don't want to be held
22   to a higher standard. I want the normal teenage boy
23   standard where I get to cuddle with my girlfriend on the bus
24   and *not* have everyone know everything about my life!
25   Is that so much to ask? Is it OK for me to pray that my
26   dad gets kicked out of church so that I can have a normal
27   life? Why couldn't he have been something cool, like an NFL
28   football player or lead guitarist in a band? Nobody would
29   care about what I did then, that's for sure!

30. Disgruntled Band Teacher

(Guy or girl)

1   Everyone wants a solo. Everyone wants to be a star.
2 Everyone wants to be first chair. But does anyone want to
3 practice? *No!* These kids must think I'm stupid. I see them put
4 their instruments in their lockers *every* day. No one takes
5 them home. Yet, miraculously, when I ask, "Who practiced last
6 night?" every single hand flies up. Well, I've heard of air guitar
7 but air trumpet? And trombone? And drums? Give me a
8 break. These kids are so lazy! And then they get mad at *me*
9 when they can't figure out how to play a song. Like it's my
10 fault they don't have a clue what each note means.

11   Don't they understand you can't get better without
12 practice? Do they really think the hour — let's face it — the
13 thirty minutes I have with them, since it takes them thirty
14 minutes to get their instruments out and get in their seats, is
15 going to make them star players? Would they expect to be a
16 starter on the basketball team if they never showed up for
17 practice? Being a quality player takes dedication and practice.
18 How come everyone understands that when it comes to sports
19 but no one understands it when it comes to band?

20   And what about forking over a little money, parents? You
21 think they can be quality players with the crap instruments
22 you buy them? They can't use a starter horn forever! They
23 need upgrades! Spend half as much on their instrument as
24 you do their fancy cell phones or their cell phone bills!

25   Does Johnny's playing get on your nerves? Get over it!
26 I'm trying to run a *band* here! If you people can't commit,
27 then get out of my room! If I don't see an instrument go
28 home with someone today, I'm quitting!

31. The Other Brother
(Guy)

1   There's one in every school, isn't there? The guy that
2   every girl wants to go out with. The jock on the basketball
3   team who scores the winning basket almost every game. The
4   guy who has muscles on top of his muscles and who has
5   every girl wanting him to wrap his strong arms around her.
6   The same guy who knows exactly what to say to a girl and
7   never sounds like a blubbering idiot or forgets his own name.

8   Oh, and don't forget that the guy dresses straight out of
9   a magazine, or looks like he belongs in one, and never, ever
10 has a bad hair day. If he did, it would only start a new
11 hairstyle around the school. Everyone copies his every move
12 like he's the ultimate "Simon Says."

13 No other guy even exists when he's around. He's like a
14 walking fly strip and every girl wants to stick to him. If you
15 are lucky enough to get a girl, you have to make sure you
16 never go within ten feet of the guy or he might decide he
17 wants her. And she would never say no to a guy like that.
18 You can't even blame her or be mad at her for it. And even
19 though you'd love to hate him for it, you can't! 'Cause he's
20 just that guy! It's not really even his fault. Can he really help
21 it if he's so perfect? How can you hate the guy who you'd
22 give anything to be?

23 Yeah, there's one in every school. The guy you want to
24 hate. The guy who has it all and then some. The guy you
25 should avoid with all your might because if you don't, you'll
26 be nothing better than a shadow — or the link between him
27 and the girls who want to date him.

28 There is no option but to stay away from him ... so what
29 do you do when that guy is your brother?

32. Vindictive Player
(Girl)

1   Nobody could believe it when the coach posted the A
2 and B team lists. Everyone told me that she must've made
3 a mistake. Clearly she'd made a mistake. There was no way
4 I didn't make the A team. I was a third-year player. One of
5 the *only* third-year players to try out. I've *always* been on
6 the A team. How could I possibly have been demoted?
7 Pushed down to the team made up of mostly sixth and
8 seventh graders! I'm in eighth grade, for crying out loud! I
9 didn't even play the B team when I was in sixth grade!

10   Coach Manning wouldn't change it either. Said my tryout
11 score wasn't in the top fifteen. So what? I had a bad tryout.
12 Probably because I hadn't even taken it seriously. I mean,
13 come on! It was a waste of my time to even try out! We all
14 knew I was going to make the A team.

15   It's like she's out to get me. She's made me the
16 laughingstock of the team. Practically the whole school. I
17 couldn't let her get away with that! Which is why they're not
18 talking about *me* any more! They're talking about her! And
19 those suspicious looking pictures that they found on her cell
20 phone! Coach Manning sure has some explaining to do now,
21 doesn't she?

22   Rumor has it she's going to get fired. Well, it serves her
23 right! She's *obviously* a horrible coach! Look what she's
24 done to me! So maybe I should feel guilty about sneaking
25 into her bag and stealing her cell phone and taking those
26 pictures, but I don't! I'm doing the school a favor. We'll
27 never win a meet with her leading the team! You bring a new
28 coach in here and we'll just see who's on the A team!

33. Cat Lady
(Girl)

1   All through science class I'd smelled it: this horrible
2 stench that reeked of bitter ammonia. I was sure it was
3 coming from the guy sitting next to me. Gerald Mason.
4 Known for greasy hair and foul-smelling clothes. Sometimes
5 there were bets about how long he went before he showered.
6 So I didn't really think anything more of it.

7   Until the smell followed me to my next class. And my
8 next. By lunchtime, there was no denying it. The stench was
9 coming from me! I couldn't believe it! How could *I* smell? I
10 always showered every morning — in fact, some days I
11 showered before bed, too! There was no way I had body
12 odor. Still, I went to the bathroom and washed my pits with
13 hand soap and sprayed a huge dose of body spray all over
14 me.

15   It worked ... for about ten minutes, and then the smell
16 came back. Filling my nostrils and making me sick to my
17 stomach! Something was seriously wrong with me! Had I
18 developed some kind of disease that caused my body to
19 reek? I got a huge lump in my throat and tears stung my
20 eyes. I used my sleeve to wipe at my sniffling nose. The
21 smell about knocked me over. I did it again. Yes! The smell
22 was definitely worse when I did that! And that's when I
23 knew! It wasn't me! It was my sweater!

24   I couldn't get out of it fast enough! Luckily I had a
25 T-shirt on underneath! It took me three more sniffs and
26 three more gags to figure out what the horrible smell was.
27 Cat pee! My sister's stupid "can't pee in a litter box like
28 normal" cat had *peed* on my sweater! It was enough to

1   make me want to puke! I'd been walking around all day
2   wearing cat pee! No wonder no one would sit by me at lunch!
3   I threw the sweater in the trash and vowed to keep that cat
4   out of my room for life! No way was I walking around like a
5   smelly cat lady ever again!

34. Surprise!
(Girl)

1   This is the worst night of my life. Worse than when I fell
2 down the bleachers during an assembly. Worse than when I
3 sang the wrong verse of the *National Anthem* at the
4 basketball game. Worse than both of those things
5 combined! Because this time — this time — it isn't just
6 about being clumsy or even forgetful — it's about being
7 *stood up* — in front of everyone! By my *best friend!*
8   I'd spent weeks planning Nicole's surprise thirteenth
9 birthday party. In fact, if you count the stuff I'd ordered
10 online — it was more like months! I spent hour after hour
11 planning, calling, scheming — just to make sure that my
12 best friend in the whole world had the best party in her
13 entire life. She'd never had a surprise party before. I wanted
14 to be the one to give that to her. And what better
15 opportunity than her thirteenth birthday? A huge milestone
16 in every girl's life. Finally becoming a true *teenager!* Not a
17 stupid pre-teen.
18   I would've let her boyfriend, Zach, in on the little secret,
19 but I know him well enough that he wouldn't keep anything
20 from Nicole! So I had it all arranged — his best friend was
21 going to pick him up and bring him here, too. Zach thought
22 he was going bowling! He would've been just as surprised
23 as Nicole!
24   Only guess what? When Blake went to pick Zach up, he
25 wasn't there! His mom said he was out with Nicole. Zach
26 stood Blake up and Nicole stood *me* up to go out on a date!
27 I've got fifty people here waiting to jump out and yell,
28 "surprise," and what do I get? A text message telling me

1   she's home sick! Home sick! She even has the nerve to lie!
2   I may never speak to her again! How could she ditch me
3   for him? Well, I guess at *this surprise party* the only one with
4   a surprised look on her face is me!

35. Junk Food Nazi

(Guy or girl)

1   There I was, minding my own business, about to sink
2   my teeth into the biggest triple cheeseburger you've ever
3   seen, when from out of nowhere — here comes this hand —
4   and snatch! The thing is grabbed away from my mouth!
5   What kind of psycho person grabs food right out of a
6   person's hand? My coach, that's who! Not only did he take
7   my burger, but he took my large fries and super-sized drink,
8   too. Not because the guy was starving to death — but
9   because the guy is a junk food Nazi! He took the whole tray
10   and dumped it in the trash!
11   Then he stood there in the middle of the restaurant and
12   lectured me about what a good athlete should and shouldn't
13   eat. As if I haven't heard that speech a million and one
14   times already. Can he even do that? Tell me what I can and
15   cannot eat? He's worse than my parents!
16   What's it really matter to him anyway? We won the game
17   last night. I played well. *And* I ate two double cheeseburgers
18   yesterday before the game! So obviously an athlete *can* eat
19   junk food and still play well!
20   I was so embarrassed, I couldn't get out of there fast
21   enough! I'm surprised they didn't call the cops on him and
22   have him thrown out! He certainly wasn't helping their
23   business! And to stand there and throw away perfectly good
24   food! Food that I paid for! I swear I have a mind to turn right
25   back around and make him pay me back ...
26   *(Pause)* What a minute! If that place is so terrible, so off-
27   limits for any serious athlete — what was Coach doing there
28   in the first place?

36. Somebody's Gotta Win!
Yeah, Right!

(Guy or girl)

1 Week after week it's the same thing. The same dreams.
2 The same endless lists of what my mom can do with her
3 winnings. She reads her horoscope, gets her palms read,
4 and even uses a Oija board sometimes, and somehow they
5 *all* tell her that she's going to win. And win big. Only she
6 never does.

7 Instead she wastes half her paycheck buying lottery
8 tickets and instant scratch-offs. The scratch-offs are quick
9 and painless, like pulling off a Band-Aid. They do not deter
10 her. When she loses at them, she's even more convinced
11 that her numbers are going to come up on the lottery. "It
12 wouldn't be fair to win both, now would it?" she asks me.

13 Sad thing is, she believes it. Down in the depths of her
14 soul she is convinced that she's going to be a millionaire.
15 She knows exactly what house and what car she's going to
16 buy and what she's going to say to her boss the second they
17 pull the balls with her numbers on them. It isn't pretty. And
18 there are some cuss words involved. She's so sure she's
19 going to win that I'm half-surprised that she hasn't gone
20 ahead and told her boss exactly what she thinks of him! But
21 luckily, so far, she's restrained herself. Thank goodness
22 because I don't know what we'd do if she lost her job! It's
23 bad enough that we don't ever have enough money for
24 groceries, or school supplies, or heaven forbid, a new shirt
25 or pair of pants. Lucky for me, holey jeans are in because
26 that's all I've got!

27 It's always worse when the pot is bigger. Doesn't matter
28 that millions more people are playing and her odds are even

1 less. That's when she starts the list of who she's going to
2 give a million to. Relatives I've never even heard of. "It'd be
3 so great to do that for so and so," she'll say. "Think how
4 surprised they'll be when I hand them a million dollars!
5 Wouldn't it be nice to change people's lives like that?"
6   Maybe. But all I'm interested in is changing *one* life!
7 Hers! I'd like to bring it back into *reality!* Mom! Listen to
8 me! You are *never* going to win the lottery!

37. Wait! Is That Her?

(Guy)

1   I remember when I was little that there was this book I
2 loved about a bird looking for his mother. He asked every
3 animal or thing he saw, "Are you my mother?" because he
4 got lost when he fell from his nest. I remember feeling sad
5 for that little bird and feeling happy that my mom was
6 always there to tuck me into bed.

7   I guess that's what you call irony. Because now, after all
8 these years, I find out that that woman was not my mother.
9 And now I am that bird. Searching. Looking into the faces
10 of strangers and wondering, "Are you my mother?"

11   Every woman I see, I analyze her mouth, her nose, her
12 eyes. Does she have my chin? What about her smile? Is that
13 the same crooked smile that I have? I don't want to think
14 these things. I know it's crazy to think these things. Of
15 course that woman walking down the street is *not* my
16 mother ... but what if she was? What if that was her and I
17 just passed her and didn't even know it? What if she's the
18 woman that I didn't hold the door open for? Or the woman
19 who cuts my hair or cleans my teeth or — God forbid — did
20 my sports physical last year?

21   How could I have gone all these years without knowing
22 that the woman who sat at my games and helped me with
23 my homework was *not* my real mother? Shouldn't I have had
24 a feeling about that? Shouldn't something deep down in my
25 soul have known that her eyes were not mine? Her blood
26 didn't run through me?

27   But then I look into those eyes, those eyes that have
28 always held love for me, and I forget that little bird. If he'd

1 found someone like the mother who "found" me, would he
2 still have been asking, "Are you my mother?" Maybe I won't
3 ever see my biological mom walking down the street. But I
4 know exactly where to find my "real" mother. She's right
5 beside me where she's always been.

38. Credit Card Craziness
(Girl)

1   I am *so* dead. When my parents figure out what I've done
2   they're probably going to call the cops on me. I can't believe
3   what I did. How could I have been so stupid? I'm not
4   normally like this. I'm the one who never gets in trouble —
5   which is probably why they trusted me in the first place!
6   But shouldn't they have known better? They're the
7   adults. Shouldn't they have known that giving a thirteen-
8   year-old girl a credit card was *not* a good idea? They know
9   how I love to shop! Why would they tease me with such a
10 temptation and expect me to be strong? I'm only human.
11 And I'm just a kid. They can't expect me to be perfect. I
12 was at the mall with my friend, for Pete's sake!
13 *(Mimics.)* "Use it for emergencies," they said. Well, what
14 actually constitutes an emergency, I'd like to know?
15 Because jeans being fifty percent off seems like a pretty big
16 emergency to me. And being starving and not having any
17 cash seems like an emergency for sure.
18 Which brings me to the second problem. *(Mimics.)* "Don't
19 tell anyone that you have a credit card," they said. Well, how
20 could I *not* tell at least my best friend? I couldn't just eat in
21 front of her, and she didn't have any money either so of
22 course I had to buy hers! And I can't help it that she ordered
23 the most expensive thing on the menu.
24 I don't know whether to tell them now or wait until the
25 bill comes in. Maybe they won't notice the charges! Maybe
26 they'll just think that they made them. Maybe they'll think
27 that *they* ate at the burger place in the mall! Oh, who am I
28 kidding? My mother hasn't eaten a burger in ten years.

1   *(Mimics.)* "Too fattening." I might as well face it, I am
2   grounded for life! And ... to beat it all, they'll probably take
3   away my credit card!

39. Designated Driver
(Guy or girl)

1   There is such a thing as the lesser of two evils:
2 situations that have two options and neither one of them are
3 good. Only, when you try to make people see that, all they
4 can see is black and white. Like life holds no gray areas.
5 Well, my life is *full* of gray areas. Which is probably why I'm
6 sitting in juvie right now while my drunk mother is passed
7 out at home on the couch. Justice is black and white. They
8 don't like gray.

9   But what was I to do? Risk my life letting my "licensed"
10 mother drive? When she'd already finished off a bottle of
11 vodka and probably half a case of beer? Face certain death
12 by letting her wrap us around a tree? So I'm only thirteen.
13 So I don't have my license yet, obviously. I can certainly
14 drive better than someone who can barely walk! I had to
15 help her to the car; buckle her in! Would it really have been
16 smarter to hand her the keys, too? I don't think so!

17   Where's the justice in this? Where's the thanks for
18 keeping an unsafe driver from getting behind the wheel?
19 Where's the sympathy for someone whose mother makes
20 him wait in the car while she bar hops night after night?
21 Instead, she gets off scot-free, and I'm the one with a police
22 record!

23   I only swerved a little to avoid that dead animal in the
24 road. Can I help it that a cop was following me? I'm a good
25 driver! Why didn't he notice all the good driving I'd done
26 before that? One little swerve and I was a danger to society?
27 He could see what state my mother was in. You think he
28 could've cut me a little slack. Looked the other way. Offered

1 to drive us home, even! But like I said, justice does not
2 tolerate gray areas. I broke the law. Black. I got arrested.
3 White. Black and white. No gray. If only life were really that
4 simple.

40. Loud Mouth Fan
(Guy or girl)

1   Everyone loves to be cheered on. No doubt about it. The
2 roar of the crowd when you spike a volleyball straight down
3 before the ten-foot line. You'd be crazy not to get swept
4 away by the chanting of your name. The adoration. It would
5 make anyone stand a little taller, walk a little prouder.

6   *(Pause)* Except when that roaring crowd is your mother
7 — the loud mouth who sounds like she has a built-in
8 megaphone. And she thinks it's totally OK to not only holler
9 at you the entire game, but to holler *nicknames* at you!
10 Some of which you haven't heard since you were still
11 carrying around baby fat. "You go, cheesecake!" "Awesome
12 serve, Tootsie Roll!" Which might actually be OK because no
13 one would actually know who that was, except she has no
14 trouble standing and pointing while she's shouting.

15   There is absolutely no doubt who her kid is. Me. For one,
16 I'm the player with the bright red face. The semi-good player
17 who wants to blend in because with all of the yelling, people
18 expect really big things. As if the star player has just
19 walked onto the court. How can you be average when your
20 fan club of *one* brings glittery signs to your games? And
21 even makes homemade T-shirts that say, "I'm the Mom of
22 Number Thirteen!"

23   It's completely humiliating. She even got yellow carded
24 by the referee once. Told her if she didn't bring it down a
25 notch he was going to ban her from the rest of the game. I
26 think it was after that game that the signs were made. But
27 the yelling didn't stop completely. She figured out the rules.
28 You can only *not* yell when someone is serving. After that,

1   it's fair game. Open season.

2   I love my mom and the support she gives me ... so how

3   do I politely ask her to *shut up*?

41. Cow Tipping —
It's Not All Fun and Games!
(Guy)

1   So maybe I'm the only one in the south who truly had no
2   idea what cow tipping really was. Seriously, would anyone in
3   their right mind really believe that someone would actually
4   try to tip a cow over? Have you ever even tried to nudge a
5   cow? It's like hitting a brick wall. I should know because
6   that's what happened last night, and now I can barely
7   breathe! I think I broke some ribs — maybe even punctured
8   a lung!

9   But how do you explain an injury like that? It's not like
10 I'm a football player. You don't get crushed bones just from
11 walking down the hall at school or staying at your friend's
12 house playing video games — which is what I was supposed
13 to be doing. I'm in serious pain here.

14   I can't believe I was so stupid. So gullible. (Mimics.) "It's
15 asleep," they said. "It'll be easy," they said. "Just run up
16 and push it," they said. Why would I even listen to them?
17 They're the same guys who put straws up their noses and
18 sucked down a glass of soda. They didn't even warn me that
19 the cow might not just "tip over." That you weren't
20 supposed to just ram the thing with all your might. It's
21 more a matter of leverage and where you push *from*. But did
22 they bother to tell me that? No!

23   Maybe I should tell my parents the truth. It's so bizarre
24 that they probably wouldn't even believe me. Or they'd be
25 laughing too hard to get mad and ground me. All I know is,
26 my sides are killing me and I'm bruised from front to back!
27 I promise I will never bother a sleeping cow ever again — if
28 I can just get a little medical attention and a huge ice pack!

42. Knock Your Socks Off!

(Girl)

1   At first I thought my boyfriend was the most polite guy
2 in the whole world. Every time he came to my house, he
3 insisted on taking his shoes off at the door. Even if he was
4 only coming in for a minute. It was so sweet ... until the
5 stench kicked in. That boy's feet smell like they belong on
6 a rotting corpse!
7   The first time it happened, I had no idea where the smell
8 was coming from. We were sitting there watching television,
9 and it kept getting worse. I would look around thinking that
10 my brother had thrown a stink bomb in on us, or that maybe
11 Mom was making cooked cabbage. I even started thinking
12 that maybe our house had been built on top of a mass
13 grave!
14   Then I leaned down to tie my shoe, and that's when it
15 hit me. Full force. Or should I say, full face! There was no
16 denying what the source was. I had to grit my teeth to stop
17 from gagging.
18   The next time he came over, I tried insisting that he
19 keep his shoes on. Told him my family wasn't fancy like
20 that. We *all* wore our shoes around the house. Twenty-four-
21 seven. He took them off anyway. Said his feet needed to
22 breathe. I wanted to agree with him. Tell him those things
23 need to breathe all right because I think they're dying! Only
24 that wouldn't have been nice. But how can I endure this?
25 How can he? It's like he's immune to his own personal
26 stench. Oblivious to the fact that his feet can clear a room.
27 My pesky brother won't even come in any more to bother us
28 — which could be a blessing. I'd rather have Donnie

1   annoying us than deal with this odor!
2   Has anyone invented a breath mint for feet? All I know
3   is, I can't wait until I catch a cold. I need a stuffy nose in the
4   worst way!

43. A.C.T. Panic
(Girl)

1   I haven't slept in three days. *Three days!* I can barely
2   keep my eyes open, but every time I try to lie down to get
3   some sleep, the panic sets in. All the things I think I should
4   know but *know* I'm going to forget start going through my
5   mind. I'll try to put myself at ease by remembering a simple
6   math formula or a simple compound like salt — NaCl — and
7   I'll go completely blank. Then I get all freaked out because
8   I know I'm going to forget absolutely everything I know when
9   I pick up that number two pencil.
10   In just five short hours I have to take the most
11   important test of my life. Who ever had this stupid idea to
12   have seventh graders take the A.C.T.? Why did they have to
13   select me? There's too much pressure. National Merit?
14   What is that? Why should I have to worry about that now?
15   I'm too young for all this stress! How can my future be
16   based on this one stupid score? What if I bomb it? "What
17   if"?! I *know* I'm going to bomb it! I'm so tired I can't even
18   remember how to spell my name. How am I going to
19   remember the difference between a verb and a pronoun?
20   *(Pause)* Darn! What's a pronoun? Is it a word that describes
21   a noun? Or a word that ends in –ly ... wait! No! It's like he,
22   she, they.
23   OK. Deep breath. I *know* that one. Of course I know
24   that one. I learned that like five years ago! They probably
25   don't even have stuff like that on the test. It's probably
26   worse! Questions over stuff that I haven't even taken yet!
27   High school courses like geometry or physics! Crazy hard
28   stuff that I won't even be able to make guesses about!

1 Maybe I should look some things up online; take some
2 practice tests or something! I've still got time!
3   Oh, who am I kidding? I've got less than five hours! I
4 might as well wake up Mom and Dad now and tell them the
5 bad news. That I'm not going to get into college. That I'm
6 going to have to work at fast food places ... or the mall ...
7 for the rest of my life. That their four-point-oh student has
8 just thrown her future down the drain! No sense letting
9 them sleep peacefully! It's time for them to accept that their
10 daughter is a complete and utter failure!

44. Scarred for Life
(Guy)

1   I have this thing about nursing homes. Not your average
2 they stink, they're creepy, or they're full of old, boring half-
3 dead people, kind of thing. But a real heart's-going-to-
4 explode-right-out-of-my-chest kind of terror.
5   It all started when I was a little kid. My parents used to
6 take me every Sunday after church to visit my grandpa.
7 After everyone hugged and said hello, my parents would
8 leave — to go get a cup of coffee or something — so that I
9 could have special "bonding time" with my grandfather.
10 Looking back, now that I'm older, I think it was so that my
11 parents could escape being with him that much longer. It's
12 like they threw me to the wolves. Sacrificed their child to
13 save themselves. I'm still trying to forgive them for that!
14   He'd always start by asking me about school, or my dog,
15 or the kids in the neighborhood. I learned early on that the
16 more I talked the less he could. So I drug out every detail of
17 my life for as long as I could. But I was only a little kid —
18 not much happening in my life. And that's when it would
19 start. The stories. He'd clasp a bony, wrinkled up hand
20 around my wrist and hold me tight to his side while he
21 regaled me with story after story. It could've been a special
22 moment between two generations. Trust me, it wasn't. My
23 grandfather had been in World War II. He'd seen things that
24 no little boy should hear about. And he had a vivid memory.
25 Right down to every gory detail.
26   I'd go home and have nightmares and beg to never go
27 back again. My parents thought I was being a selfish brat —
28 not wanting to waste my Sunday with an old man. They

1   dragged me there week after week. Left me alone with him,
2   time after time. My stories got longer and longer. But it
3   didn't matter. I was at his mercy, and he knew it.
4   My grandpa died last month. I'm no longer forced to
5   spend my Sundays listening to R-rated gore fests about the
6   war. I wish I could say I miss those days with my grandpa,
7   but the truth is, I don't. I wish just once he could've told me
8   stories that didn't end in bloodshed and rotting body parts
9   scattered on a field. I'm glad my dad never went to war
10 because this is one family tradition that stops right here!

45. Soul Pollution

(Guy)

1   I wish stupid kids who go around shooting people would
2 stop telling everyone what kind of music they listen to!
3 Because of them, my parents are freaking out! Telling me
4 that the music I listen to is going to affect my brain — cause
5 me to do something or be somebody I don't want to be. I'm
6 *not* a moron! I can listen to a song and not want to do what
7 it says! These psycho kids are giving punk music a bad
8 name. How come not *one* of these school killers can be a
9 Barry Manilow fan? Or what about a Carpenters fan? Isn't
10 that enough to make someone go ballistic?
11   I'll tell you why those kinds of kids aren't out bringing
12 an Uzi to school — they're too busy writing suicide notes!
13 Because I'd kill myself if I had to listen to that sappy stuff!
14 How can they possible tie music to someone's behavior? It's
15 not sending out secret messages, people! It's just music!
16 Words in a melody. Make-believe! Get it? *(Sarcastically)* Not
17 even if you play it backward!
18   *(Mimics.)* "Garbage in. Garbage out," my parents say.
19 Can I help it if they don't understand the music of today?
20 Besides, their music wasn't any better. It might not have
21 had such a kicking beat, but there has been violence, sex,
22 and drugs in music since the sixties! What ever happened
23 to freedom of speech? They can't make me listen to that
24 drivel they listen to! I don't care if they call it "soul
25 pollution"! I have a right to pollute my soul if I want to!
26 *(Pause)* Maybe ... just to prove a point ... I'll load the Bee
27 Gees to my iPod and then I'll go knock off a bank or
28 something! Then — maybe for once — they won't be able to
29 blame what I did on a bad rap song!

46. Christmas Scrooges — with a Purpose

(Girl)

1   My parents have completely lost their minds. They've
2   gone all earthy, save-the-world kind of thing, and they're
3   taking my sister and me down with them!
4   No presents! *No presents?!* Are they crazy? You can't
5   have Christmas without presents! What will we do
6   Christmas morning? Sit around and look at each other? Talk
7   about world hunger, find a cure for cancer? What are they
8   doing? Trying to buy a straight ticket to heaven? Don't they
9   know that God cannot be bought?
10   This is the most ridiculous, over-the-top thing I've ever
11 heard. You don't just stop Christmas. *(Mimics.)* "We have a
12 responsibility." Well, what about their responsibility as
13 parents? Their responsibility to their *children* — not the
14 world! I don't *want* to spend Christmas day ladling soup for
15 the poor. I don't *want* them to spend *my* Christmas gift
16 money on toys for kids or care packages for the military. I
17 don't *want* to buy a cow, or a goat, or even a chicken for a
18 backwards, underprivileged village!
19   Don't we get a say in this? Don't we get to decide if we
20 want to be charitable with our gifts? I don't mind helping out
21 the poor. Remember — I did help raise money last year for
22 that well they built in Uganda. But what's it going to hurt if
23 I have Christmas, too? No one's going to know!
24   This is a two-part holiday! You have to have the *giving*
25 and the *receiving!* It's just not the same without it! We're
26 not saints! We're two girls with needs and desires. I've
27 waited all year to ask for a television for my room! *All year!*
28   I'm not a bad person. I'm not! But seriously, Mom and

1   Dad — *no* Christmas? We might as well give up *all* the
2   holidays! *(Pause)* No, wait! I was kidding! You cannot take
3   away Easter, too!

47. Allergic to Love

(Girl)

1 *(Very dramatically, arms thrown open wide)* I think I'm
2 allergic to love! *(Pause)* OK, maybe that's a little over the
3 top. After all, I'm not really even sure if I love Frank. We've
4 only been dating a few months. It's a tad too early to start
5 throwing the "L" word around, isn't it? And we are a little
6 young — only in eighth grade.
7   But if it's not love I'm allergic to, it must just be him!
8 Every time we get close to each other, I break out in a rash.
9 Big red welts pop out all over my arms and legs! Like a
10 swarm of mosquitoes just ate me for lunch. It's horrible.
11 And they itch, too. I'm sure you can imagine how lovely I
12 must look — like a swelled-up, flea-bitten dog or something,
13 scratching my heart out.
14   So I'm pretty sure that you can safely say that he's not
15 in love with me yet either! But I think we could have a shot.
16 We have so much in common. And he makes me laugh like
17 nobody ever has before. He says he doesn't care about my
18 "reaction" — which is nice of him — but then, he's not the
19 one itching, is he?
20   Who am I kidding? How can I have a relationship with a
21 guy when I can't be within ten feet of him! Which my dad,
22 by the way, thinks is perfectly acceptable! He thinks the
23 more distance the better. In fact, he didn't want me to have
24 a boyfriend until high school anyway! But that's just
25 ridiculous!
26   Frank's tried changing everything: his cologne, soap,
27 shampoo, toothpaste. He even tried *not* wearing deodorant.
28 Whew. Thank goodness that wasn't it! I think I'd rather have
29 welts!

1   What else can there be? Is it coming from his pores? I've
2   tried all kinds of allergy medicine, but taking an
3   antihistamine is like taking a sleeping pill for me! I slept all
4   through the movie and I still broke out in welts!
5   This is *so* unfair! I may have found Mr. Right, and I'm
6   allergic to him!

48. Straight Ticket to You-Know-Where
(Guy or girl)

1   I know the difference between right and wrong. I know
2 the Ten Commandments and what I should and shouldn't
3 do. I *know* that "thou shalt not steal" is not optional. So
4 why, when the offering plate was passed right under my
5 nose, did I think for a second that it was OK to "borrow" a
6 ten-dollar bill from it?

7   That's right! You're looking at the lowest form of human
8 life possible. Even people in prison are better than me.
9 There has to be a special place in you-know-where for
10 people who steal from a church!

11   I don't know what came over me. It's not like I *had* to
12 have it. So what if I didn't pay the deposit on the youth trip
13 this week? I could've turned it in late. Or — worst case
14 scenario — not been able to go. That would've been
15 disappointing, but not the end of the world. Nothing could
16 feel worse than the guilt I'm feeling now.

17   What am I supposed to do? How can I make it right? Put
18 a ten-dollar bill back in next Sunday? What if I paid interest
19 on it? What about a twenty? That's double the money.
20 Surely God wouldn't be mad if I gave back twice as much
21 as I took! Think about it: The money would've sat in the
22 bank all week making practically nothing in interest. So I
23 "held" it for a while, and now the church makes a huge
24 profit! It's almost as if I did something better for the church.

25   *(Pause)* Yeah. That's lame. I know it. There's no excuse
26 for what I did. Thank goodness we don't practice all those
27 ancient laws, or someone would be cutting off my hand!

28   There's really only one thing I can do. I can take another

1   ten-dollar bill and turn it into something good. Food for the
2   poor. A toy for a kid in a hospital. Something really special.
3   Something to show God how sorry I am. Believe me, the
4   next time the offering plate comes my way — I will not treat
5   it like an ATM!

49. Halloween Horror
(Guy)

1 Halloween night is supposed to be full of harmless
2 pranks. It's been that way for generation after generation.
3 Toilet-papered trees, rotten eggs on cars, maybe even a
4 stolen bag of candy from an unsuspecting kid. So there was
5 nothing inherently wrong with my friends and me heading
6 out for a few holiday tricks.
7   We knew exactly which houses we wanted to go to. Mean
8 Mr. Parker's house was number one on the list. He'd ratted
9 us out to our parents just a few weeks before for barely
10 sideswiping his mailbox. I had a whole six-pack of toilet
11 paper with his name on it. Then there was Ms. Hanky, the
12 woman in Keith's neighborhood who called the cops on us
13 for being too loud at his back-to-school party. A dozen eggs
14 and she was good to go.
15   The last house we threw in at the last minute. Complete
16 strangers that, as far as we knew, hadn't ever done
17 anything to us. But they had a whole porch full of lit
18 pumpkins. Just asking for trouble. How could we resist?
19   We had already smashed two of the pumpkins when the
20 trick went bad. Flames from one of the candles caught
21 Keith's pants on fire. He kicked his leg around in panic and
22 knocked two more lit pumpkins over. More flames shot up
23 his leg. Within seconds his pants were completely engulfed
24 in flames. So much for non-flammable clothing. It was like
25 his pants were made of the toilet paper we'd thrown earlier.
26   We were all yelling — especially Keith — and it alerted
27 the people inside. They came running to see what was going
28 on. The same people we were in the process of "tricking"

1 tackled Keith to the ground and put out his pants. Those
2 same people rushed him to the hospital so his third degree
3 burns could be treated. Those same people called Keith to
4 check on him every day for a week. They never even yelled
5 at us.

6   Halloween may be a night of tricks and treats. But from
7 now on — for me — it's nothing but treats!

50. Why Would Anyone Trust Me?
(Guy or girl)

1   See this? This wreck of a room? This is me. Cluttered.
2 Unorganized. A slob. Someone who smells his clothes to
3 see if they're clean because everything I own is on the floor.
4 I have food that is actually growing underneath my bed. My
5 parents know this. My friends know this. The few who have
6 dared to come over know that I haven't seen my floor in
7 about three years.

8   So knowing all of this — knowing me — why would
9 anyone entrust me with hundred-dollar concert tickets?

10   That's right. I've got five hundred dollars worth of
11 tickets somewhere in this mess, and I can't find them. Five
12 hundred dollars! My parents are going to kill me. My friends
13 are going to kill me. *I'm* going to kill me! I don't have that
14 kind of money. In fact, I don't have *any* kind of money! Do
15 I look like a guy who's motivated enough to have a job? I
16 don't think so!

17   Why did I ever offer to buy the tickets online for
18 everyone? Why was I dumb enough to have them mailed to
19 this house? Why would my parents be stupid enough to let
20 me use their credit card? Why would I even begin to think I
21 should bring the tickets up here — to this black hole —
22 when they came in the mail?

23   Well, there's really only one thing I can do. *(Pause)* Move.
24 Take on a new identity. Start in a new town, in a new school
25 where no one can find me ... *(Pause)* ... Shoot! I have
26 absolutely no idea where my suitcase might be!

51. Summer Dad

(Girl)

1   I've walked into the twilight zone. Some sort of parallel
2 dimension where I'm still, like, five years old or something.
3 Get a load of this place! Pink walls, white lace curtains! A
4 canopy bed, for crying out loud! Does *anyone* even have
5 those any more? And look! A "Hello Kitty" radio and
6 matching table lamp. Who can live without those?

7   This room hasn't changed one iota since my parents got
8 divorced — six years ago! It's like a shrine or something. I
9 know I only get to come once every summer, but come on,
10 Dad — seriously! Do I look like I belong in this room? How
11 much does a can of paint cost?

12   I know every father wants to pretend his daughter is still
13 his "little girl," but this is completely ridiculous! In fact, it's
14 way *past* ridiculous! I feel like I should be wearing pigtails
15 and knee-highs when I come here.

16   Look at me! I am not the pigtails and knee-highs kind of
17 girl. Never have been. This stuff has got to go. I've spent my
18 last summer in the Twilight Zone! This weekend I'm having
19 a yard sale and then I'm painting this room a color I can live
20 with. Anything to cover up this Pepto-Bismol pink. It makes
21 me want to throw up!

52. No One Wants Her ...
and That's the Way I Like It!
(Guy)

1   I have this problem. It started out as something I could
2   control, but then it grew into this huge issue that totally
3   consumed me. Day and night. I was totally obsessed. I went
4   from being the loving, over-protective, "isn't that sweet"
5   boyfriend into a scary, over-zealous, stalker boyfriend! Her
6   parents even called the police on me!
7   But all I could think of was how pretty she was and how
8   every guy in school would want to go with her and why
9   would she possibly want to be with a guy like me? I didn't
10 deserve her. How could I possibly keep her? Of course, I
11 couldn't. Crazy psycho behavior turns a girl off.
12 I figured with this insane jealousy tendency inside of
13 me, I was destined to be alone forever. And then it hit me.
14 The uglier the girl — the easier it would be. I sought out the
15 ugliest chick in school and I asked her to be my girlfriend.
16 It started out as an experiment — you know, kind of like
17 an alcoholic who makes his first trip back into a bar — sees
18 if he can stand the temptation? It worked! We walked down
19 the hall together, and I didn't have a shred of worry that
20 every guy was checking her out. It was amazing! So freeing!
21 I started to relax. Even enjoyed having a girlfriend that I
22 could hang out with and not be looking over my shoulder the
23 entire time!
24 That's when it happened. I fell in love. Hard. I became
25 the alcoholic that had to have the drink. I started seeing all
26 the wonderful qualities my girlfriend had: her sense of
27 humor, the way she waited for me after class, the sweet
28 notes she wrote me. Once I figured out how lucky I was, I

1   started worrying that other guys might figure it out, too.

2   Now I'm back to where I started! Green-eyed and

3   obsessed — watching her every move! You think I could talk

4   her into being home-schooled? Because that's the only way

5   this relationship is going to work!

53. Ben Franklin's Regrets

(Guy)

1   You think you're doing your country good. Spending your
2 time inventing things to make everyone's life easier. Down
3 the road, you realize that somehow you've done just that.
4 In fact, you've made everyone's life a little too easy! This
5 modern world is nothing short of pathetic!
6   Look at these people! They have more electronic
7 gadgets than a top-notch scientist or a whole section of the
8 government! They have a gizmo for everything! Heaven
9 forbid they should do something for themselves. Even their
10 toothbrushes are electric! Is moving your arm up and down
11 really such a chore?
12   These people are letting their minds go to mush. The
13 worst contraption is that picture box they call TV. You sit in
14 front of that, and it's like going into a time warp or
15 something. I watched one man sit in his chair an entire day!
16 At least twelve hours wasted in front of that loud obnoxious
17 thing! He didn't even care. Like he'd wasted an hour instead
18 of all day!
19   If I'd known I'd be contributing to the likes of this mess,
20 I never would've discovered electricity. I can tell you that for
21 sure. Look at all the trouble it's caused. It's made people
22 get farther apart rather than closer together. Nobody seems
23 to talk anymore. I haven't heard a lively discussion in
24 decades! There are too many distractions! Too much one-
25 sided entertainment!
26   And books! Don't even get me started on that! Doesn't
27 anyone know how to read a good book any more? Heaven
28 forbid someone should actually read a newspaper — not

1   just line their cat litter box with it! Doesn't anyone realize
2   how hard we fought for freedom of speech — and they're not
3   even paying attention to it!
4   Well, the good thing is — every cloud has a silver lining.
5   At least with this bunch of loafers, there won't be anyone
6   smart enough to invent anything new! Knowing these lazy
7   morons, they'd invent something to live, eat, and breathe for
8   them!

54. Skinny Pants Are *Not* My Thing!
(Guy)

1   Where is it written that to be a skateboarder you have to
2 wear skinny jeans? I've been skating all my life wearing
3 exactly what I want, and now it's like you're not a "real"
4 skater unless you wear pants that couldn't fit on my little
5 sister! It's ridiculous. When I skate in them, I can barely
6 bend my knees they way I need to, and the waistband is so
7 tight on my stomach that I can't breathe! How am I
8 supposed to skate wearing pants that won't let me move or
9 breathe? They cut off my circulation and make my legs go
10 numb!
11   We're skaters. We're supposed to be cool. These pants
12 are the least cool thing a guy could ever wear. They belong
13 on a girl! I'm not saying we need to go back to the whole
14 saggy pants thing — obviously not, because then the pant
15 legs get caught in your wheels, and you sure don't want that
16 to happen! Just ask Tommy Jenkins! He broke three ribs
17 and his right arm trying to skate in a pair of pants that were
18 at least three sizes too big!
19   But isn't there a happy medium in there somewhere? A
20 pair of pants that doesn't look like I painted them on? A pair
21 of pants that doesn't take me twenty minutes to even fit
22 into? I'm serious! I wish you could've seen me this morning
23 trying to get into these things! I was acting like a seriously
24 deranged animal. My big feet can barely fit through the
25 bottom leg holes, and I had to lie on my floor just to get
26 them zipped up. It was comical really. I was getting so
27 desperate I thought I was going to have to have my mom
28 come and help me! Can you picture that? Well, I can't, and

1   I don't want to!

2   *(Pause)* So if I hate them so much, why am I wearing

3   them, right? Well, I'll tell you why ... I'm a skater. Through

4   and through. And if this is what all the skaters are wearing

5   then so be it! I'll shove my fat legs into these skinny jeans,

6   and I'll show them I can skate as good as anyone — even

7   when I can't feel my legs!

55. The Grand Entrance
(Girl)

1 I'd always heard of the importance of making a grand
2 entrance, but I never thought it would happen to me! I'm not
3 talking about a gorgeous gown, late to the ball, everyone's
4 looking at you kind of grand entrance either! No, this was
5 much more dramatic than that!

6 There I was in the new dress I'd just snagged from the
7 clearance rack a few hours earlier. New shoes — not even
8 flip flops — which says a whole lot right there! And a new
9 hairdo I'd copied out of one of those hairstylists' magazines
10 when I was waiting for Mom to get her hair cut and colored.

11 So, all in all, I was looking pretty great. Maybe even a little
12 too great, since we were only going out to eat and to the
13 movies. But it was the first time John and I were actually
14 going on a real date and not just hanging out somewhere, so
15 I'd decided to put a little extra oomph into the night.

16 I heard his car door slam — his mother always made him
17 come to the door and get me — so I started down the stairs
18 to greet him. I was hurrying because I wanted to surprise him
19 by being ready and not making him wait, like usual.

20 My foot slipped in my new shoe and I stumbled down the
21 stairs. Like, with the force of a train running off its tracks. I
22 slammed into the unlatched screen door and landed
23 sprawled out on the front porch — inches away from my
24 John's feet.

25 I jumped up to find my knees scraped and throbbing,
26 blood on the hem of my new dress, a broken heel, and a
27 completely shocked look on John's face.

28 Certainly I had made a grand — or should I say a *very*
29 *big* — entrance!

56. Mr. Right Is Mr. Wrong

(Girl)

1   Leslie's friend who works with Chuck's friend who has
2 basketball practice with Tim's cousin said that Tim told him
3 that he was planning on asking me to the Eighth Grade
4 Graduation Dance! Me! The girl who has had a crush on the
5 guy since fourth grade! Me! The girl who can barely make
6 eye contact with the guy of my dreams! *Me!* The girl who is
7 about to have the date of a lifetime!

8   Every time I see Tim coming, my legs go weak and I feel
9 sick to my stomach. I've planned what I'll say over and over
10 in my head. I want to appear flattered but not too desperate.

11   I don't know what's taking him so long! He's seen me
12 exactly seventeen times since I found out from Leslie's
13 friend through Chuck's friend through Tim's cousin that he
14 was going to ask me! The dance is only a week away now!

15   What if he changed his mind? Why would he change his
16 mind? I haven't done anything to make him change his
17 mind! I haven't even spoken to him! What kind of guy
18 ditches a girl before he even asks her out?

19   Omigosh! What if I turned down Sam — and Brian — for
20 nothing? What if now, because of Tim, I don't have a date?
21 I'll look like a loser! Like a girl who couldn't get a date! No
22 one will believe that other guys asked me and I turned them
23 down!

24   Ooooh ... I should've known better than to listen to
25 Leslie just because she has a friend who works with
26 Chuck's friend who has basketball practice with Tim's
27 cousin! He might not have even meant me! *Omigosh!* He
28 didn't even *mean me!*

29   *Aaaahhhh!*

57. Alphabetizing Is *Not* for Sissies!
(Guy)

1   Some people might call it a problem — an issue that one
2 might want to address with a certified professional, maybe
3 even consider taking medicine to correct. I say — why?
4 Since when did making order out of chaos become
5 something to be condemned? As if living in an orderly world
6 was the cause of insanity instead of the other way around?
7   So I alphabetize everything — my CDs, my DVDs, my
8 books, and my boxes of cereal — big deal! What is so wrong
9 with knowing exactly where to find something? Is it saner to
10 frantically search through thrown-about items, therefore
11 wasting time and energy?
12   Why is it that my friends and family members find it
13 humorous to rearrange my things? Do I, on the other hand,
14 find humor in trashing their stuff? Of course not! I would
15 never subject someone to a life of disarray! Nor would I find
16 it the least bit funny! Chaos is *not* a goal, it's a symptom!
17 A symptom of underlying issues — laziness, inferiority, low
18 self-esteem! Slobs on the inside, complete messes on the
19 outside!
20   I am not the one in need of therapy, people! It is *you* —
21 the cluttered and the lazy — who need to wake up and
22 examine yourselves!
23   It is not too late! There is more to life than the chaos
24 you have created! I promise you this — you, too, can have
25 a life of order and organization! You, too, can alphabetize!

58. Why Can't You See That I'm Switzerland?

(Girl)

1　　I don't want to know what Sarah said about you at last
2　night's football game. I don't care what look Teresa gave you
3　when you passed her in the hall. I don't give a darn that
4　Sarah invited every cheerleader but you to her party on
5　Friday night. I especially couldn't care less if Teresa only
6　wore that outfit because she saw you buy it first.
7　　Why can't you understand that I am friends with *both* of
8　you? I do *not* want to be your mediator, your go-between,
9　your interpreter, or your counselor! If you want to say
10　something to each other — say it! I am tired of being caught
11　in the middle. I like you both. Not one more than the other.
12　The *same*. I will not choose between you or voice an opinion
13　on who is right or wrong or who looks better in a stupid
14　skirt!
15　　I am Switzerland. Get it? Neutral to the end. Do not
16　come to me with your petty problems, snide remarks, and
17　disagreements. Do not ask me to pass along hateful
18　messages or notes of apology. You are both capable of
19　delivering those yourselves.
20　　If you want to know the truth, you're *both* acting like
21　brats. Childish, backstabbing, hateful little snobs who have
22　nothing better to do than tear each other apart! In fact, I
23　think you both deserve each other!
24　　So there — you wanted my opinion, now you've got it!
25　You're both wrong!
26　　*(Pause)* What? You're mad at *me* now? Oh, come on!
27　　Wait! Teresa!
28　　*(Turns the other way.)* Sarah! You know I didn't mean it.

1   Come on! You've got to tell Teresa that I didn't mean it!
2   She'll listen to you. Wait! Maybe if I wrote her a note ... you
3   could give it to her ...

59. You Gonna Eat That?

(Guy)

1   Sometimes I think I need to tie a stupid ribbon around
2 my finger or stick a note to my forehead. Something.
3 Anything to help me remember all the stuff I have to
4 remember! For three days now my lunch account balance
5 has been zero. For three days I've told myself, "Self, don't
6 forget lunch money tomorrow." And for three days, I've
7 walked into school completely oblivious to the fact that once
8 again I do *not* have lunch money in my pocket or backpack.
9 Not until I walk into the lunchroom does it cross my mind
10 that I've forgotten again.
11   That means three days of no lunch. By law they have to
12 give you something — a peanut butter sandwich. Well,
13 guess what? I'm allergic to peanut butter! So, not much
14 help there!
15   They don't care that I'm starving! They would never
16 treat an elementary school kid this way. You let one of them
17 go hungry and the parents would sue the bricks off the
18 school. But you let a middle school kid go hungry and you've
19 "taught that kid something about responsibility." What a
20 bunch of bull. If it'd taught me anything, I would've
21 remembered the money on the second day, now wouldn't I?
22   Do you know how embarrassing it is to have to ask a
23 classmate for food? Like, "Hey, you gonna eat that?" Three
24 days in a row! I know everyone thinks I'm poor instead of
25 forgetful. It's so humiliating. Well, today is it. The last day I
26 will forget. I'm writing a note on my hand. I'm calling my
27 house and leaving a message on the answering machine.
28 I'm leaving a voicemail on my phone and setting an alarm.
29   Tomorrow I will not beg for food!

60. Dating Tips from King Henry
(Guy)

1   OK guys, listen up! I don't know what's wrong with
2 young guys today, but you've got it all wrong! You're more
3 whipped than a horse on Derby day! Girls have got you
4 wrapped tighter than caramel on an apple! You're being led
5 around like you're on a leash!

6   Since when does a woman rule the relationship? It's
7 high time you stepped up to the plate and put your foot
8 down! Tell her who's in charge.

9   Not right off the bat, of course. That would be dating
10 suicide. You're going to have to woo her a little. Buy her
11 some flowers. Jewelry is good. Walk her to class. Carry her
12 books. Truth is, you've got to treat her like a queen! Make
13 her think you live to serve her.

14   But that's only step one, and that's where you morons
15 seem to have gotten stuck! You can't keep up that kind of
16 pace forever. You're making the real guys look bad.

17   Step two is to keep her guessing. You guys jump into
18 this whole "I love you" thing way too fast. You go down that
19 road, and you're stuck for good. You might as well have four
20 flat tires, 'cause you aren't going anywhere ... and she
21 knows it!

22   Lastly, if all else fails and you think she's getting away
23 — let her go! You don't need her! You're too young to date
24 anyway! Come on! You're only in middle school! You've got
25 your whole lives to be tied down to a ball and chain!
26 Otherwise, you'll end up like me, shouting, "Off with her
27 head!"

61. More Than a Broken Bone
(Girl)

1   I heard the snap. In fact, I'm pretty sure the whole gym
2 heard the snap. They saw the girl trip and come flying at
3 me. They knew before I did what was going to happen. I was
4 still focused on getting the ball. Sure that I could make it in
5 time. I didn't know there was danger until it was too late.
6 Until I was flat on my back, my leg twisted in such a way
7 that the audience gasped.
8   There was no question whether it was broken. The angle
9 of my leg and the bone pushing at the skin left no doubt. I
10 was taken out on a stretcher. The pain was so intense I
11 could think of nothing else.
12   *(Pause)* The thinking came later ... after the talk with the
13 doctor. And the surgeon. The break was bad. They had
14 doubts that I would play volleyball to my full potential ever
15 again. Even with therapy they couldn't guarantee that I
16 would ever return to normal. The pins in my leg would make
17 sure of that.
18   My parents were as crushed as I was. It wasn't only a
19 broken bone. It was a broken dream. It was the beginning
20 of the season. I was a starter! A key player! My sister was
21 already playing Division One college volleyball and I was
22 going to follow in her footsteps! My lifelong dream. My
23 injury, of course, sent that dream spiraling down the tubes!
24   But I'm not going to let this beat me! I'm not. I'm going
25 to prove those doctors and the coaches wrong. You watch!
26 One day you'll see me playing college ball — that's a
27 promise!

SECTION 2
DUOLOGUES

Movie Maniac
(1 Guy, 1 girl)

1   62. DONALD'S VERSION
2
3   DONALD: Let me give you a little advice. Don't ever
4   meet up with your girlfriend in a dark theatre. In the lobby?
5   Sure. Out in the parking lot? OK. But never, ever think that
6   you know what your girlfriend looks like in a pitch-black
7   theatre. Even when she's whispering, "I'm over here," and
8   you *think* you know exactly where "over here" is.
9   There I am, thinking I'm sitting next to my girlfriend —
10   offering up a quick kiss of apology for being late and wham!
11   I'm getting slapped upside my head by some chick who
12   decides to scream the word "Pervert!" out to the whole
13   theatre.
14   I try to apologize, ears ringing from where she's slapped
15   me, and what do I do? Stumble on top of *another* chick in
16   the seat beside the screaming slapper! Put my hand right
17   down in her — well, let's just say I got a handful of popcorn
18   from the bag that was sitting in her lap. She was *not* happy,
19   to say the least.
20   At this point, everyone else in the theatre is either
21   laughing their heads off or pulling their cell phones out to
22   call the cops on me. I can no longer hear my girlfriend —
23   either because it's so loud in there or she's stopped
24   speaking to me because she doesn't want anyone to know
25   I'm with her.
26   Over and over I apologize as I make my way to the end
27   of the row. I don't even care where my girlfriend is now. I
28   just want to slide down into a seat and ride out the

1 commotion. The first bright scene that lit up the place and
2 I was out of there. I don't care if I never go to another movie
3 again.

4

5   63. KAYLA'S VERSION

6

7 KAYLA: You will never believe this! Last night, I was
8 sitting with my friend Tina watching the previews of this
9 really scary movie when all of a sudden this pervert guy
10 plops down into the chair beside me and kisses me! Out of
11 nowhere! It all happened so fast that I didn't even see it
12 coming!
13   Of course I screamed and slapped him! Who knows what
14 he was going to do next! Well, actually I *do* know — because
15 he barely got around me before he was groping my friend,
16 Tina, in her chair! She was pinned to her seat and he was
17 all over her! Like a maniac. Gross!
18   Everyone started laughing — yes, that's right —
19 laughing! Can you believe that? A guy is groping girls in the
20 theatre and people think it's funny! My legs were shaking, I
21 was so scared. Tina and I called the police, but by the time
22 they got there the guy was long gone. Snuck out before
23 anyone could get a good glimpse of him.
24   It's made me terrified to go to the movies. Right now, I
25 don't care if I ever see another movie again!

Trash Picker

(2 Girls)

64. KIM'S VERSION

2

3   KIM: It's totally clear now. My mother has completely
4 lost her mind! I've always thought she was on the edge, but
5 tonight — tonight she has jumped right over the cliff! I'm
6 seriously thinking about calling the paramedics! Someone
7 has to do something. *(Turns to side as if talking to Mom.)* You
8 think I'm kidding, Mom? Well, I'm not! Look, I'm getting my
9 phone out right now. I'm dialing the ...
10   *(Pause — then mimics the mother.)* Yeah, I *know* this is the
11 third retainer I've lost. Yeah, I *know* they cost almost five
12 hundred dollars each. Yeah, Mom, I *know* that money
13 doesn't grow on trees! But dumpster diving? At night? With
14 a flashlight?!
15   *(Looks over the edge of the dumpster. Shudders. Holds hand
16 over nose and mouth.)* Omigosh! Can you smell that? There
17 might be dead bodies in there. Seriously. You hear about
18 that on the news all the time. *(Very sarcastically)* OK, Mom,
19 maybe not *all* the time! But it happens! Do you really want
20 your sweet, innocent, little daughter stumbling across a
21 decomposed hacked-up body? *(Pause)* What do you mean
22 I'm not that sweet? You're the one making your own flesh
23 and blood dig through the trash like a homeless person.
24   *(Looks around.)* What if someone sees us? They'll think
25 you don't feed me. That's right! They'll think we're too poor
26 to buy food. They'll think the Hammond family is so bad off
27 that they have to eat out of the trash! Surely your reputation
28 is worth a stinking five hundred dollars!

1   **65. MOTHER'S VERSION**

2

3   **MOTHER:** OK. So maybe it is a little drastic. Making my

4 daughter dig through the dumpster at this time of night —

5 well, at any time, really. But I'm so sick of her blase

6 attitude when it comes to losing her retainer. She thinks

7 nothing of me having to shell out five hundred dollars every

8 time she throws it in the trash. How many times have I told

9 her not to wrap it in a napkin and stick it on the tray?

10   *(Mimics daughter.)* **"But that's *gross*, Mom! Nobody wants**

11 **to see my retainer when they're trying to eat. It's like looking**

12 **at Grandma's teeth! Gag!"** Well, I don't care what other

13 people want to see. But guess what? That's not her only

14 option. Every time I re-buy the stupid thing they give her a

15 case. That's right — an actual *thing* she could put it in —

16 instead of the trash! She could pop it out, stick it in the

17 case and then put it in her purse! But oh no! That's just way

18 too inconvenient for her. It's so much easier to throw it in a

19 wad of napkins and then toss it in the trash!

20   It's so much *easier* for *Mom* to just take *another* half day

21 off work to go to the orthodontist. Oh yeah, that's easier for

22 *everybody!*

23   So that's why we're out here in the middle of the night,

24 digging in the trash — well, she's digging, I'm watching.

25 There's no way I'm digging through that garbage. There's no

26 telling what's in there. But I'm sure there aren't any dead

27 bodies! She thinks I'm falling for that one? Who's the crazy

28 one here?

29   And so what if people see her? Maybe they *will* think

30 we're that desperate! If I have to keep buying her retainers,

31 I may have to get another job anyway! That'll make the

32 neighbors talk!

Text Addiction
(2 Girls)

1   66. SARAH'S VERSION

2

3   SARAH: Three thousand? In a month? Now that's a
4 record! No, I'm not being smart, Mom. I just can't believe I
5 sent three thousand text messages in thirty days! Don't
6 look at me like that! Hey! When you think about it, that's
7 only an average of one hundred a day. Considering how
8 many friends I have, that's only like ten messages apiece.
9 That's nothing! I know this girl who sent over five thousand
10 messages in a month. Her bill was over twenty-five pages
11 long!
12   I don't know why you're getting so upset! We've got
13 unlimited text messaging! I could send ten thousand
14 messages if I wanted to. *(Pause)* No, Mom, of course I'm not
15 saying I'm going to send ten thousand text messages. Yes,
16 I *know* the phone is a privilege and that you can take it
17 away. Yes, I understand that you made it through middle
18 school, high school, *and* college without ever sending a text
19 to someone. *(Under breath)* That's because they barely had
20 cell phones back then.
21   *(Pause)* Oh, come on! I was kidding. Why can't you ever
22 take a joke? What? No! You can't take my cell phone! I
23 haven't done anything wrong! How will my friends get ahold
24 of me? How will I know what's going on? What if something
25 important happens? Jason is supposed to ask Andrea out
26 this weekend. I'll be the absolute last person on earth to
27 know!
28   You can't do this to me! What if I promise not to text for
29 a whole week? Well, uh … I could never make it a whole

1 week, Mom! What about a whole day ... starting now! All the
2 way until tomorrow. Come on, that's fair! *(Pause)* This is
3 prime time texting! Parents heading off to bed ... no, of
4 course it doesn't matter if you're in bed or not. No! I'm not
5 texting anything bad! No! You can't read the messages in
6 my sent box! That'd be like reading my diary! Come on,
7 Mom! Be reasonable! I promise I'll cut back. Just don't take
8 my phone!
9
10 <center>67. MOTHER'S VERSION</center>
11
12 MOTHER: This is the most ridiculous thing I've ever
13 seen! Look at this! They must've killed a whole tree to print
14 this bill! Three thousand text messages in a month! *Three*
15 *thousand!* What could you possibly have to say in three
16 thousand text messages? I'm surprised you haven't worn
17 the buttons off your phone.
18 No, it doesn't matter that we have unlimited text
19 messaging! It's the principle of it, Sarah! The fact that
20 you're wasting all this time with your fingers glued to that
21 phone and doing nothing else! You haven't even begun your
22 summer reading project, and school starts in a week. A
23 week! Maybe you can write your paper to your teacher in *text*
24 *messaging!*
25 No, I will not calm down. You know having a phone is a
26 privilege that we give you, and we can take it away at any
27 time. Having a cell phone is *not* a necessity. I certainly made
28 it through all of my school days and some of college without
29 ever having one! *(Pause)* You think that's funny? You think
30 I'm too old to have had a chance to have a cell phone? Well,
31 they've been around a lot longer than that! I chose not to
32 waste my money ... but why would you care about money?
33 You don't pay the bill, do you? Well, maybe that's the
34 problem! Maybe if you started babysitting and paid for this
35 outrageous "free" text messaging as you call it, you'd think

1 differently! That "free" to you costs me an extra twenty-nine
2 ninety-nine a month!
3   That's it! Give it here. Anyone who has time to text
4 message three thousand times a month has time to do
5 some extra chores or make some money babysitting or
6 cutting lawns! That's right! You're not too good to do some
7 honest labor! You can have this back when you can afford it!

Hey, She's *Your* Friend!
(2 Girls)

68. BRITTANY'S VERSION

2

3   BRITTANY: In the history of unfair — this takes the
4   cake! Why should I have to ask Kori over to hang out just
5   because she's my mother's best friend's daughter? I don't
6   involve my mother in my friendships, why does she have to
7   involve me in hers? Can't the freak stay by herself? Why
8   does she have to come along just because her mother's
9   coming over? Can't they trust her alone? Does she hit the
10 bottle when no one's home? Or maybe she steals things
11 from her own house! Or maybe she has wild parties and
12 trashes the house! Why would my mother want me to be
13 friends with someone like that?
14   The girl is E-M-O. She's got more chains on her than the
15 state penitentiary! Of course my mother is forcing me to be
16 friends with her. She can't possibly have any friends of her
17 own! Next she'll be making me tutor her because I'm sure
18 she's flunking every subject in school. Probably burns
19 books in her bedroom late at night as part of some funky
20 dark ritual. I'm going to be stuck with this chick in my life
21 forever! How could my mother be friends with someone who
22 has a daughter like that? These kids don't just accidentally
23 turn out this way, you know!
24   They've probably got some deep, dark terrible family
25 secret and my mother is too gullible to see it. The mother's
26 probably going to sucker her in for everything we've got!
27 Steal our identity! Clean out our savings! I don't care how
28 innocent she looks, the daughter is a dead giveaway that

1 something is *not* right with that family!
2   Well, I will not be a part of it! Mom can force me to let
3 the creepy chick in, but she can't force me to talk to her.
4 We'll sit in silence all night. I'll read a book. She can sit and
5 watch me if she wants. Maybe I'll leave out some magazines
6 so she can get a clue about how *normal* people dress. All I
7 know is, if she thought I was going to be her new best friend
8 — she is sadly mistaken!
9
10   **69. KORI'S VERSION**
11
12   KORI: This is great. Just great. I had a perfectly fine
13 night planned out with my friends and now my mother is
14 forcing me to go hang out with "Little Miss Plastic," Brittany
15 James. That girl is so fake, I'm surprised her eyes aren't
16 painted on. And that laugh — how am I supposed to survive
17 that valley girl laugh? It makes me want to puke! I swear the
18 girl doesn't have a brain in her head! But with a chest like
19 she has, being smart certainly doesn't seem to be a
20 requirement.
21   How could my mother become friends with a family like
22 that? They're, like, right out of the movies! One boy, one
23 girl. Check. One dog. One cat. Check. One sports car. One
24 minivan. Check. One white house and picket fence. Check.
25 Gag me! The woman even wears dresses! When she's not at
26 work! I didn't think real people even did that! My mother
27 hasn't shaved her legs in ten years! What could she possibly
28 have in common with this woman?
29   This is so ridiculous! Can't baby Brittany stay home
30 alone? What she going to do — gag up her dinner? Or — I
31 don't know — watch an R-rated movie? Aaaaahhhh! The girl
32 can't be trusted! Why do I get babysitting duty? I didn't sign
33 up for this friendship! *(Pause)* Oh, I bet I know what it is. The
34 girl's probably failing school! She isn't just blonde on the
35 outside, I can tell you that! Dear old Mom's offering for me

1   to tutor her — for free! As a perk of being her friend! I can't
2   believe this! I've been sold out by my own mother!
3   Well, she can force me to go over there, but she can't
4   make me help her! We can sit in silence all night for all I
5   care. The chick can earn her own grades. I work hard to
6   keep a four-point-oh; I'm not handing over that knowledge
7   for free! To a girl who couldn't name a continent if she had
8   to!

Mother Has *Not* Got It Going On!

(2 Girls)

2

3   STACY: Don't get me wrong. I love my mom. A lot. And
4 for the most part, we get along really well. Especially since
5 my dad left us a few years ago. I guess the whole
6 abandonment thing kind of bonded us together. And I'm
7 glad that my mom has decided it's time to "move on." Or
8 "hit the dating scene," as she likes to call it. But my mom
9 is not hitting the scene — she's demolishing it! Like a
10 tornado that rips apart a town.
11   She's gone totally wild. Partying all hours. Dancing all
12 night. The woman has more bags under her eyes than my
13 dad even bothered to pack! She's not only got the candle lit
14 on both ends — she's melted the whole darn stick!
15   But her being a party animal isn't even the worst part.
16 It's her clothes. She's gone from normal "mom wear" to
17 underwear model! Seriously. I can totally see her thong
18 sticking out of the back of her way-too-tight jeans. *Thong!*
19 My mother is wearing a thong! How gross is that? No one
20 wants to imagine their parent wearing things like that! And
21 her clothes aren't any better. Her shirts are either so short
22 you can see her stomach — which, OK, Mom, *yuck!* People
23 can see your stretch marks! Ugh! And if it's not so short you
24 can see skin, it's see-through the whole way around. And
25 then she'll wear some fancy lace, black bra underneath it.
26   And her makeup is completely off the charts. She's
27 caking on so much foundation, I could probably etch my
28 initials into her face. Doesn't she remember those famous

1   words she told me, "less is more?" Well, *less* makeup and
2   *more* clothes would be nice! It's getting embarrassing.
3   Yesterday at the parent-teacher conference, my history
4   teacher sat down beside my mom to look at papers — and
5   he touched her hand several times and smiled. And she
6   smiled back! I tell you what, she would never be acting this
7   way if Dad were around. I never thought I'd say this, but if
8   she doesn't straighten out soon, I'm going after him!
9
10   71. MOTHER'S VERSION
11
12   MOTHER: You know how some mothers and daughters
13   completely clash all the time? Especially when the daughter
14   hits those rough teenage years? Well, I am so happy to say
15   that it doesn't have to be that way! My daughter and I are
16   best friends. We have been for years! We hang out all the
17   time, and we tell each other absolutely everything! She's
18   been totally cool about me dating again. See, her dad took
19   off a few years ago — but really, it's the best thing that
20   happened to us! We've become so close because of it. I
21   sometimes wonder if she would've been the typical "I hate
22   my mom" teenager if we hadn't gone through so much
23   together.
24   But she is so awesome! She helps me get ready to go
25   out. She's always offering suggestions about what I should
26   wear, or how I should do my hair. She'll even do my makeup
27   if I let her! Funny thing is, she is *so* conservative! It's like
28   she's the parent and I'm the teenager! I'll pull out something
29   to wear and she'll say things like, "Ummm ... that's a little
30   revealing, don't you think, Mom?" When did she become so
31   prim and proper? She's trying to dress me like a grandma!
32   And I'm only forty! I'm in the prime of my life. Look at the
33   movie stars who are my age! Do you see them dressing all
34   frumpy? Heck no! And if they can do it, why can't I?
35   I probably should be a little more careful around her

1 school, though. Just yesterday her teacher tried to hit on
2 me! I could tell it made Stacy very uncomfortable. I wouldn't
3 want anything jeopardizing our relationship. *(Pause)* But I
4 wonder if she's considered the benefits of having a mother
5 date her teacher — straight A's for sure!

BFF Is a Pig!
(2 Girls)

1   72. SUSAN'S VERSION

2

3   SUSAN: I absolutely adore my BFF! She is so sweet and
4   thoughtful, and she's always there for me. I can't tell you
5   how many times I've called her crying about boy issues or
6   parent issues! And she always listens and never acts like
7   I'm bugging her. She's been at every volleyball game I've
8   played in and she always cheers the loudest. I guess you
9   could say she's absolutely perfect.
10   *(Pause)* Except that she's a pig. A complete and total
11   slob. I'm talking food on her floor, chips in her bed, and
12   garbage that overflows from her trash can. Her clean clothes
13   are mixed with her dirty ones, and you would need a shovel
14   to dig something out of her closet. It is totally disgusting. I
15   feel the need to use antibacterial cleanser every time I'm
16   there. Who knows what germs are festering in her bedroom.
17   I swear she's got six kinds of fungus growing in there!
18   I guess I didn't mind it so much when we were little. I
19   mean, we were still playing in dirt, for Pete's sake! So who
20   cared if her room wasn't much better? But somewhere along
21   the line, I started noticing how utterly disgusting it was at
22   her house. Whenever I left there, I felt grimy and gross like
23   I couldn't do anything else until I went home and showered.
24   But how do you tell your BFF that the smells in her room
25   make you want to puke? She thinks we're growing apart
26   because I never want to hang out there any more. I know
27   I've hurt her feelings by saying no when she's invited me
28   over, because now when I ask her to my house, she always

1 makes excuses. I don't want our friendship to go down the
2 tubes because of this, but how can I stay some place that
3 isn't fit for pigs?
4
5   73. MEGAN'S VERSION
6
7   MEGAN: My BFF is the best in the world! Last year
8 when I broke my leg, she carried my books to all of my
9 classes and made me get-well cards almost every day. When
10 we were in fifth grade and my parents got divorced, she
11 stayed at my house for two whole weeks! She cried almost
12 as much as I did! I don't know what I'd do without her! Ever
13 since we were little we've been inseparable.
14   *(Pause)* Until lately. She used to come to my house
15 almost every day and she always spent Friday or Saturday
16 night — sometimes both nights! We always hung out here
17 because my mom is so much better about leaving us alone.
18 We could stay up all hours and do pretty much whatever we
19 wanted. Now, Susan is always inviting me over there.
20   *(Rolls eyes.)* Ugh. I don't want to be mean about it — but
21 come on, her house is so ... stiff. Like you can't have a thing
22 out of place! Susan has white carpet in her bedroom! White!
23 Now what does *that* tell you? No one in their right mind has
24 white carpet! And she makes her bed with those tight
25 hospital corners. I feel like I'm going to suffocate in that
26 thing! I can't even move my legs. And get this! We can't eat
27 in her bedroom. *No one* in her house eats in their bedroom.
28 Not even the parents! Not even a snack or a glass of water!
29 It's worse than being in prison.
30   It's so much better at my house. I have *zero* rules when
31 it comes to my room. My mom says it's my space and I can
32 live in it how I want! I eat in my room more than I do the
33 kitchen! Why wouldn't I? I can watch television, talk on the
34 phone, do homework — whatever — and not have to leave
35 my room for a second! It's totally awesome!

1   I don't know why Susan wants me to stay over there
2   now. The place has *no* personality. It's cleaner than a
3   hospital. Her mother must dust and vacuum every single
4   day? How can Susan stand to live that way?

Ride of My Life!

(2 Guys)

1   74. DENNIS' VERSION

2

3   DENNIS: That was the most exciting, exhilarating,
4   mind-blowing thing I've ever done! Talk about the ride of
5   your life! That was it! The speed! The cold air hitting your
6   face! That near-collision with the truck! Omigosh! It was
7   like straight out of a movie! We could probably become
8   stunt men because of that!
9   You got it on tape, right? Tell me you got it on tape! I'll
10   plaster that thing all over the Internet! I'll be — we'll be —
11   famous, William! The two of us on every computer screen in
12   America. In the world! And all caught first-hand, from *our*
13   point of view, the speed, the truck — right there — about to
14   hit us! All caught on tape with your ... *(Pause)* ... Dude!
15   Where's your camera? Where's the camera?!
16   *(Pause)* Omigosh! Tell me you didn't drop it! Tell me you
17   got the most amazing stunt ever pulled in the history of
18   homemade stunts! It will never be as perfect as that — ever
19   again! I mean, the truck practically *grazed* us, dude! Do you
20   know the timing on that? One second slower and we
21   would've been smeared all over the highway! It would've
22   taken dental records or DNA testing to identify us!
23   *(Pause)* This is unbelievable. *(Shaking head back and forth*
24   *like he can't believe it)* Well, there's only one thing left to do.
25   Find the camera. Make sure it still works and re-create the
26   stunt. That's right. Hook the sled back up to the truck and
27   do it again! This time I'll hold the camera!
28   It's what they say in show business: Ride of Our Lives
29   — Take Two!

1   75. WILLIAM'S VERSION
2
3   WILLIAM: That was the scariest, most terrifying, mind-
4 blowing thing I've ever lived through! I can't believe I'm still
5 in one piece! My body is shaking all over and I think I'm
6 going to vomit. I now know what they mean when they talk
7 about your life flashing before your eyes! It was all happening
8 in slow-mo and zoom speed at the same time! I know I felt
9 the truck's tires graze the side of my arm!
10   We could've been killed! Smeared like gum to that guy's
11 tires! My heart is pounding so fast I still might die from a
12 heart attack! Then, to top things off, in the middle of all
13 that, I lost my new video camera! I'm pretty sure I chucked
14 it when I went to shield my face from the impending impact
15 of the truck. How it didn't hit us is completely beyond me.
16   It's nothing short of a miracle! I don't know why I let
17 Dennis talk me into these things. Why would I even believe
18 that hooking a sled up to a truck and then being slung down
19 a snow-covered hill toward a four-lane highway would *ever* be
20 a good idea? Thank goodness the rope snapped, or we'd be
21 highway road kill for sure!
22   You'd think he'd be grateful that we're alive — that
23 somehow by the grace of God, we survived that disaster!
24 But no! He's ticked off because I didn't get the whole thing
25 on tape! He doesn't even care about my camera. He just
26 cares about the footage.
27   And now — now — he wants to do it again?! Has he
28 completely lost his mind? You don't cheat destiny twice, my
29 friend! Well, he can go the next time without me — or my
30 camera!

An End and a Beginning
(1 Guy, 1 girl)

76. EMMA'S VERSION

2

3 EMMA: It all happened so quickly. I remember seeing
4 the headlights — they were so bright — blinding me as they
5 came toward me. Then there was complete darkness and a
6 silence like none I'd ever experienced before. Too quiet. Too
7 dark. Like nothing that could possibly happen in the real
8 world. No feeling. No sound. No smell. Nothing.
9   Maybe that's when I knew. When I realized that
10 something had gone terribly wrong. I wasn't in the
11 passenger seat of my friend's car coming home from the
12 game any more. I wasn't laughing with my friends. I wasn't
13 turning up the song on the radio. I wasn't singing at the top
14 of my lungs. I wasn't doing any of those things ... because
15 I was dead.
16   It wasn't supposed to happen that way. I was too young.
17 I still had eighth grade graduation, high school, prom, and
18 college, and getting married, and having kids. I was
19 supposed to do something important; make my parents
20 proud; help out a friend. I wasn't supposed to die on the
21 side of the road because someone made a bad decision.
22 Because drinking and driving don't mix.
23   I wasn't supposed to ... but I did. There's no turning
24 back. For me, that's not so bad. The things I see and feel
25 and do now are incredible. Beyond imagination. Better than
26 prom, or marriage, or anything else in the world.
27   But what about those I left behind? Are their hearts
28 healing? Do they have faith in what's happened to me? Are

1 they celebrating my life or mourning my death? Are they
2 able to move on? How can I ever let them know that I'm OK?
3 That one day, I will see them again. Please, just let me give
4 them a sign. Let them know they haven't lost me.
5
6   77. TAYLOR'S VERSION
7
8   TAYLOR: I still can't believe she's gone. I still smell her
9 here in the house. Still see her face, hear her laughter, all
10 around me. How can we go on without her? We were a family
11 of four — not three. We can't even sit at the table for dinner
12 now. It's too obvious there. The empty chair. The empty
13 space.
14   Sure, we can shut her door and pretend that her room
15 isn't empty. Pretend that maybe she's still in there, listening
16 to music, talking on the phone with her friends, leaving dirty
17 clothes piled up on the floor. But it doesn't change anything.
18 She isn't in there. She isn't anywhere. She's gone. For good.
19   The trial starts in a few weeks. I hope they fry the guy!
20 A life for a life, I say! The papers have tried to paint this sob
21 story of his life — like I care! Why should he get an excuse?
22 An out for his behavior? He made the choice to drink those
23 beers — all *six* of them — before he got in his car and *killed*
24 my sister! Why should I feel sorry for him? Why should I care
25 if his parents left him or beat him or if the kids at school
26 made fun of him? Big freaking deal! Get over it! Quit
27 blaming everyone else for your mistakes! Nobody forced you
28 to get behind that wheel! Nobody poured that alcohol down
29 your throat!
30   *(Pause)* Everyone's talking to me about forgiveness.
31 Trying to convince me that Emma would want me to forgive
32 him. What a bunch of bull! Do they really think Emma is OK
33 with her life being cut so short? That she liked feeling the
34 impact of his car slamming into her at eighty miles an hour?
35 That she's OK with never going to high school or college or

1   getting married? Emma wanted at least five kids! She would
2   never forgive the guy who robbed her of that!
3   *(Pause)* It's crazy, but sometimes I think I feel her with
4   me. I'll hold something of hers, and this extreme feeling of
5   peace will come over me. Like she's telling me that she's
6   OK. I wish I could know for sure that it was true. That it's
7   not just my imagination feeding my brain what it wants to
8   feel. Maybe ... if I knew she was in a better place ... not just
9   dead and buried ... I could move on. Not forget. But not hurt
10 so bad.
11   Emma — I love you. I miss you more than anything. I
12 sure hope you have gone on to heaven — because we —
13 Mom, Dad, and me — we feel like we've gone to hell.

New Girl/Old Girl
(2 Girls)

2

3   MARLENE: Do you have any idea how much I hate my
4 mom right now? How tired I am of "starting fresh" in a new
5 town and a new school just so she can climb the stupid
6 corporate ladder? I'd rather she settle for a corporate
7 stepstool! How much higher does she have to climb? How
8 much more power does she have to have? Ever since Dad
9 left us, she's been on this kick of proving herself to the
10 world or something.
11   I'm sick of being the new girl in school. Eating alone.
12 Walking to class alone. Being stared at and whispered
13 about. And that's if I'm lucky. Most times I'm completely
14 invisible — not even worth the time it takes to check me
15 out. To wonder where I've come from or what I'm all about.
16 At one school I went a whole month before anyone even
17 spoke to me. Teachers included. I took up space. That's
18 about it.
19   Mom promised me we're staying here until I graduate
20 high school. Yeah, right. We'll be lucky to make it a whole
21 year here. I can't wait until I *do* graduate. Four more years
22 and I'm free. Off to college. Anywhere I want to go. Mom
23 can move all she wants — I'm picking a place and I'm
24 staying put. That's right. Same place all four years! Four
25 years! Maybe I'll even make some friends. Get to know
26 some people. Figure out more than just the main streets
27 around a town.
28   Maybe I'll even get bored a little — complain about how
29 there's nothing to do there. It'll be great! I'll have seen

1 everything there is to see, done everything there is to do! I'll
2 *know* people. People will *know* me. For once in my life I
3 won't be invisible!
4
5   79. SHELIA'S VERSION
6
7 SHELIA: See that girl over there? The one sitting all
8 alone? The one sitting there in complete and total peace? I
9 would give anything to be that girl! No one bothering her,
10 yakking in her ear about boys, teachers, clothes, and every
11 other minute detail of their lives. I am so sick of everyone
12 coming to me with their problems. They think that just
13 because my father is the minister of the town's largest
14 church that I — by default — care about each and every one
15 of them. That I have to *like* every single one of them!
16   Yeah, yeah, I know — love thy neighbor and all that jazz!
17 But come on, I'm not a saint! I cannot possibly be expected
18 to care about every one of these trouble-laden kids! But of
19 course they expect me to. I've practically been raised with
20 these people. I see them on Wednesdays, twice on Sundays,
21 and at my house all the time in between! It's like we've got
22 a revolving door — everyone come on in! Don't worry that
23 we never have a family moment to ourselves!
24   Can't I have a moment to myself? Just one second when
25 I don't have to smile and nod and listen as if I truly care? I
26 don't want to be the girl that everyone can talk to. I want to
27 be *that* girl. The one that *no one* talks to! Hasn't anyone
28 ever heard that "silence is golden"?
29   I can't wait until I turn eighteen. I'm getting out of this
30 town and moving to a big city where no one will know my
31 name. I'll blend in with the masses and become a nobody!
32 It'll be so great! For the first few years I won't even try to
33 make friends. I'll be a hermit! A recluse! I'll be the weird
34 apartment girl that never speaks, or waves, or smiles at
35 anyone! Maybe then I can live in peace!

Love Stinks!

(1 Girl, 1 guy)

1   80. BRANDI'S VERSION

2

3   BRANDI: Boys are so dumb! It's amazing they can even
4 function — they are *that* dumb! They walk around all cool-
5 like, thinking that every girl in school wants to go out with
6 them. Acting like they run the school. Then if they actually
7 do get a girlfriend, they are completely clueless about how
8 to act. It's ridiculous!
9   See that moron over there? That's Jake. My boyfriend.
10 He bugged me for three whole months to go out with him.
11 Left me notes in my locker, in my books, even in my gym
12 shoes! Listen to this: *(Pulls out note)* "I look at you and my
13 insides turn to butter." Corny, I know. And look! I've got a
14 ton more of them! I could probably wallpaper my bedroom
15 with them! And if that wasn't enough, he got every single
16 one of my friends to put in a good word for him.
17   So finally I said yes. I mean, he was kind of growing on
18 me. And even though he is obviously dumb when it comes
19 to having a girlfriend, he is kind of cute. Just look at him.
20 That wavy brown hair. Those deep blue eyes.
21   Things would be perfect except now he won't even look
22 at me, much less talk to me! We're together on paper only.
23 I seriously have not been within ten feet of the guy since I
24 said yes. And we have *three* classes together! How lame is
25 that? We spoke more when we were just friends! I think the
26 guy is scared of me!
27   Well, he can have all these corny love notes back
28 because as of this minute, this relationship is officially *over!*

1
2
3
4
5
6
7
8
9
10
11
12
13
14
15
16
17
18
19
20
21
22
23
24
25

81. JAKE'S VERSION

JAKE: Have you ever wanted something really, really bad? Like so bad that it eats at your insides? Well of course you have! Who hasn't? What would Christmas be like if we didn't obsess over getting things that we think we just *have* to have, right?

But have you ever really, really, *really*, wanted something — maybe even dreamt about getting it — and then you get it and *whoa!* You're over it? Like maybe it wasn't what you wanted after all. Or maybe by the time you got it, you'd already found something else you wanted even more?

Well, see that girl over there? That's Brandi. My girlfriend. The girl I just *had* to have for three whole months. She's all I thought about twenty-four-seven. I wrote her more notes than Beethoven put in his symphony! Ha! Get it? *Notes?* In a symphony? Sometimes I just crack myself up ...

(Pulls back together.) Yeah, well, anyway ... I really, really wanted her to go out with me, only now that she said yes — I'm kind of over it. It's like I won the race; got the prize; posed with the trophy. Boring. Done. Over.

Thing is, how do I tell the girl that I begged to go out with me that I don't want her anymore?

Hey! I know, maybe I'll write her a note!

123

Ghost Talker

(1 Guy, 1 guy or girl)

1   82. TIM'S VERSION

2

3   TIM: I just don't know what I'm going to do! I've got

4 ghosts bothering me twenty-four-seven. They think that just

5 because I *can* hear and understand them that I *want* to talk

6 to them.

7   Do you have any idea what it's like to see dead people

8 first thing in the morning and last thing at night? It doesn't

9 make for pleasant dreams, I can tell you that!

10   Life was so much easier before I got this gift — or rather,

11 this curse! They won't leave me alone. I can't even leave my

12 house. They're always there — waiting for me at the door.

13 Ready to talk, talk, talk. Do you know how many times I've

14 been caught talking to "thin air"? I swear they're going to

15 commit me. I'm going to spend the rest of my life locked up

16 in the looney bin because these stupid ghosts won't just *go*

17 *into the light!* How come they need me to help them figure

18 it out? I'm thinking it isn't rocket science! Leave the living

19 alone and go be with people of your own kind ... you know,

20 the other people with maggots coming out of their heads.

21   Why can't they see that I just want to be left alone? I

22 don't know how I can be any clearer. If I wanted to talk to a

23 ghost, I'd kill myself!

24   *(As if addressing a "ghost" in the room)* **Look. You don't**

25 **talk to me, and I won't talk to you, OK?**

1
2
3
4
5
6
7
8
9
10
11
12
13
14
15
16
17
18
19
20
21
22
23
24
25
26
27
28

83. GHOST'S VERSION

GHOST: You wait and wait all your life — OK, maybe all your death — for someone to come along who can actually see you and then, bam! There he is! Right in front of your transparent face!

So, of course I want to talk to the guy. I haven't had a conversation with a real human being in a zillion years. OK, maybe just a couple of decades! Do you know how hard it is to be stuck here and have *no one* to talk to? I've been going out of my mind! It's not like there's help for that kind of crazy, either — you know what I'm saying? You see any dead psychiatrists running a practice around here?

But what does this joker do? Acts like he can't see me or hear me. Completely, one-hundred percent ignores me. Tries to look right through me — which, okay, isn't exactly impossible! But I saw his face! I saw him react when he came into the room and I was hanging out there. He looked right at me! He did! Oh, he looked away real quick, but it was too late! I saw him! *I saw him!*

Then, bam! Out come the headphones. Now he's got his eyes closed and the music cranked so loud, he wouldn't be able to hear me if I was rattling chains in his ear! As if I could or even would do something as lame as that!

Well, he's got to take them off sometime. When he does, have I got an earful for him! He might as well get used to it. Me and him — we're going to be stuck like glue for a long, long time!

SECTION 3
TRIOLOGUES

Dress Code Disaster
(3 Girls)

1   84. A TEACHER'S VERSION

2

3   TEACHER: It's about time the school board took a stand
4   around here and made some changes that really matter! For
5   years now I have watched the skirts get shorter and the
6   necklines get longer! You see more skin walking down the
7   hall in this school than you see in the swimsuit edition of
8   *Sports Illustrated!* I'm not kidding either! Most girls today
9   have zero modesty!
10   And the guys are no better! Their pants are so loose I
11   can't tell you how many times I've been "accidentally"
12   mooned! They can't even bend over to pick something off
13   the floor without their pants falling down around their
14   ankles! And since when did showing your underwear to
15   everyone become acceptable?
16   A uniform is just the answer. Button-up shirts that they
17   will have to actually *button up!* There's a thought all in
18   itself! These kids today think that buttons are purely
19   decorative! They wouldn't dream of actually using them!
20   Well now they won't have a choice. Rule is all three buttons
21   or you're in violation of dress code!
22   The best part is that they'll have to wear belts with their
23   pants! No more flashes in the middle of class! We might
24   actually accomplish something every now and then without
25   all of the clothing malfunctions!
26   Sure, they're whining now. Begging for their rights. Well,
27   get over it! For years they were warned to clean up their act
28   or we'd clean it up for them! But it always got worse, not

1 better. Starting Monday, the decent and morally dressed are
2 reclaiming this school!
3
4   85. CANDI THE PREPSTER'S VERSION
5
6   CANDI: O-M-G! This is *so* unfair! I-D-K why they want us
7 to look like a bunch of clones! Does anyone care about
8 fashion any more? How can they possibly expect us to be
9 individuals if we all look exactly the same? It is so *lame.*
10 And what are we supposed to do with our current
11 wardrobes? Do they even have a clue how much a shirt like
12 this costs? Feel the material! It's soft. Nothing at all like the
13 scratchy cheap stuff they're wanting us to wear! I'll probably
14 break out in a rash! I'll be so busy itching, I won't be able
15 to concentrate. Those B's I've worked so hard to get will be
16 gone — like snap! And whose fault will it be? Theirs! The
17 dumb school board and principal and even the dumb
18 students who actually voted for this disaster!
19   They're taking away my right to express myself! They're
20 even talking about rules on hair bows! Can you believe that?
21 What the heck is wrong with ribbons in your hair? Somebody
22 tell me! It's not like a ribbon separates the social classes —
23 they sell ribbon at Wal-Mart, people! Heck, I'll buy everyone
24 a ribbon myself!
25   Oh, and the absolute worst part — khaki pants! And not
26 just any kind of khaki pants, but the kind like my mother
27 wears! They're worse than mom jeans! The waist comes up
28 so high I can't even see my belly button! Do they have any
29 idea how horrible it is to make kids our age wear something
30 so hideous! The style is so yesterday! So the *day before*
31 *yesterday!*
32   Well, they've left me no choice! Until this stupid rule is
33 repealed — I'm getting home-schooled! T-T-Y-L!

1   **86. KAREN THE ANTI-PREP'S VERSION**
2
3   KAREN: This is so hilarious! You should see all the little
4 prepsters scurrying around, gathering in their little preppy
5 groups, and completely freaking out over the fact that come
6 Monday they'll be wearing a super-great blend of eighty
7 percent cotton and twenty percent polyester — all woven
8 together to make a very plain, no-nonsense, three-button
9 shirt! The same shirt that we'll *all* be wearing in a lovely
10 array of blue, white, or gold!
11   It's so great! You should see how they're panicking! It's
12 like, O-M-G, their little brains are completely tied to their
13 outfits! Like, "O-M-G, how can we even think without our
14 mall clothes on?" Or, "O-M-G! How will anyone tell us apart
15 any more?" "My B-F-F won't even recognize me!"
16 Aaaaahhhh! *(All of this is said with great sarcasm and*
17 *mocking.)*
18   I've even seen a few girls crying. *Crying!* Over stupid
19 clothes! Not poverty, or hunger, or war! But the fact that
20 their pants aren't going to be as skin-tight as before! And
21 that — ewwww — their belly buttons are going to be hidden
22 in their pants instead of trying to peak out from under their
23 too-short shirts! Sniff, sniff. O-M-G. I think I might cry!
24   We're not — and by that I mean the non-preps, of course
25 — exactly excited about the whole uniform idea either. But
26 you don't see us flipping out about it! Walking around crying
27 and such! If you want to change something, you don't just
28 sit around and cry about it. You do something. That's why
29 we're organizing a protest! That's right. We're going to stand
30 up for our rights! And not because of fashion, either! This is
31 a violation of our freedom of speech! They can't turn us into
32 clones! Come Monday morning, we're on strike!

Middle School or Prison —
You Be the Judge
(3 Guys)

1   87. DISGRUNTLED TRANSFER STUDENT'S VERSION

2

3   DISGRUNTLED TRANSFER STUDENT: Going to school
4 here is worse than being in prison! I'm serious. The teachers
5 actually walk us to classes instead of letting us get there on
6 our own. Sound familiar? Kind of like when the prison
7 guards walk the convicts around? They might as well carry
8 guns and strip search us! I'm pretty sure these teachers
9 would have no problem shooting us for getting out of line,
10 or, heaven forbid, talking when we aren't supposed to!

11   They give detentions for everything! Miss one
12 assignment — detention! Late for school — detention! Pass
13 a note in class — detention! No warnings any more. Just
14 straight to detention! There are so many rules around here,
15 I'm pretty sure that prisoners *do* have more rights than us!
16 They definitely have more freedom — and they're behind
17 bars!

18   I've never been to such a restrictive school before! These
19 teachers don't let anything slide. You can even hear the
20 announcements at the end of the day. I was probably in
21 fourth grade the last time I heard those. No teacher has
22 control in those last few minutes of school. But these
23 teachers do! Right up until that final bell rings! Even then
24 they expect us to go to our lockers and the bus in an orderly
25 fashion! An *orderly fashion?!* Are you kidding me? I've got
26 exactly three minutes to get to my locker, grab my stuff,
27 and get to the bus! But don't let them catch you running for
28 it! Or — you got it — *detention!*

1   I swear, I wish we'd never moved here. Things were way
2 better at my old school!

3

4   88. RELIEVED TRANSFER STUDENT'S VERSION

5

6   RELIEVED TRANSFER STUDENT: This is the best
7 school I've ever been to! And, let me tell you, I've been to a
8 lot! My dad gets a new job about every other year. So I
9 know what I'm talking about when I tell you that this school
10 completely rocks! Sure, it's a little strict. Maybe even a lot
11 strict. But that's the best part! I can actually concentrate in
12 class now. These teachers actually have control.
13   They don't put up with all the junk my old teachers put
14 up with. At the last school, teachers were actually afraid of
15 the students. Some even had guards in their classes, and
16 that didn't even stop the chaos! Do you have any idea how
17 frustrating it is to be a good kid in an environment like that?
18 The teachers spent so much time dealing with disruptions
19 that they never had time to go over anything. You had to
20 learn stuff all on your own. I might as well have been home-
21 schooled! I've taught myself everything anyhow! Problem is,
22 I'm not good at it. I'm a student, not a teacher! And so my
23 grades were slipping.
24   It's going to be so much easier here! Now I can take
25 notes and do assignments and study — in peace! The
26 teachers explain everything instead of me trying to figure it
27 out, and those troublemakers who used to rule the class —
28 they're taken out immediately. No warnings! One mistake
29 and they're out of there! In-school detention was the best
30 idea ever! Put all the class clowns together, I say! If they
31 want to talk and cut up, do it somewhere else!
32   You know what, this year, I may actually be able to get
33 a four-point-oh!

1   **89. THE DETENTION STUDENT'S VERSION**

2

3   DETENTION STUDENT: The rules around this school
4   are driving me crazy! It's not that I'm a rebel or major rule-
5   breaker or anything. In fact, up until this year — my first
6   year in middle school — I had never been in trouble in my
7   life. Never even seen the inside of a principal's office.
8   Now I've had three detentions in a week! I'm not a bad
9   guy. I'm not! I'm just forgetful. But that's a major sin
10   around here. Forget your homework: detention. Forget to get
11   your parents to sign something: detention. Forget anything
12   and you might as well pack up your things because you're
13   off to detention. It's so ridiculous! It's like they think that
14   just because we've graduated from elementary school we're
15   supposed to act like adults!
16   My parents think that I've gone bad all of a sudden. That
17   middle school has turned their normally good student into a
18   rebellious pre-teen set on self-destruction! They've grounded
19   me from everything! They've even checked my backpack to
20   see if I'm smoking cigarettes or doing drugs! All because of
21   a couple of detentions! It's like they've completely forgotten
22   that I'm not a bad student!
23   Where's the trust? Where's their faith in me? Why can't
24   anyone see that I'm not trying to get in trouble! Maybe I've
25   got a really young version of Alzheimer's or something.
26   Shouldn't they be helping me instead of giving me
27   detention? Besides, what's that prove? It just puts me in a
28   room with a bunch of troublemakers, and then I can't get
29   *anything* done!

Mama's Boy
(1 Girl, 2 guys)

1   90. HEATHER'S VERSION

2

3   HEATHER: My boyfriend's parents are driving me crazy.

4 They treat Chris like he's in Kindergarten instead of eighth

5 grade! He has a seven-o'clock curfew on school nights and

6 a generous — get this — ten-o'clock curfew on the weekend.

7 Ten-o'clock! We can't even get to the early movie and back.

8 Oh no, instead we have to go to the daytime matinee with

9 all of the little kids and old people. It's so ridiculous.

10   But that's not even half of it! They monitor his e-mails

11 and text messages. Not just your occasional obligatory I-

12 need-to-make-sure-you're-not-doing-drugs kind of thing —

13 but *every* message. Phone calls, too. We have absolutely no

14 privacy. It's like they're his prison guards instead of his

15 parents.

16   Even when they do let him out of their sight, he has to

17 constantly check in. I swear he text messages his mother

18 more than he does me! One night he forgot to text her to

19 say that we got to the movies OK — which is *less than five*

20 *miles away and my parents drove us* — and she actually

21 came to the theatre! Got in her car and drove over ... like a

22 crazy stalker or something!

23   I mean, come on, it's one thing to love your kid — to

24 even worry about your kid — but those apron strings they've

25 got tied to him are strangling both him and me!

1
                          91. CHRIS'S VERSION

2

3   CHRIS: My girlfriend is driving me nuts! She wants to
4 spend every stinking moment with me. It's like she thinks
5 she's the only thing in my life. I'm supposed to totally stop
6 seeing my friends, playing my guitar, or even play one
7 second of my favorite video game. And now she hates my
8 parents and they haven't even done anything!
9   It's all my fault, though, 'cause I started using them as
10 an excuse to get away from her. Don't look at me that way.
11 I know it's lame to hide behind your parents, but what else
12 could I do? Heather would have me going over to her house
13 every day.
14   She wants to *do* stuff all the time, too. Like eat out and
15 go to the movies. I think we've seen every movie that's out
16 right now. Well, I don't have that kind of cash. I'm too young
17 for a real job, so I've got to use my allowance, or my yard
18 mowing money, or do extra chores around the house. Well,
19 heck with that! I'm not spending all my money on her! I
20 can't afford nighttime movie prices. They're almost double
21 what the matinee costs! And come on, it's the *same* movie.
22 Who cares if we see it during the day or at night? It's dark
23 in the theatre — just pretend it's night out!
24   Oh — and my parents don't read my e-mails or text
25 messages either. I just told her that to get her to stop
26 writing me so much! I had over a thousand texts from her
27 last month! It's ridiculous. It's like she has to tell me every
28 stupid thing that's going on. She even texts me about the
29 weather. And then she gets mad if I don't say something
30 sweet at least a hundred times a day. Well, a guy can only
31 take so much talking in a day anyhow. I had to do
32 something!
33   Don't get me wrong. I care about Heather. I do. She'd be
34 the perfect girl, too, if she'd just leave me alone every now
35 and then!

1   92. FATHER'S VERSION
2
3   FATHER: I think there's something wrong with my son.
4   See, he's got this really cute girlfriend and he never wants
5   to spend time with her! Aren't guys his age supposed to be
6   obsessed about things like that? Begging to go out all the
7   time? I know he's still young, but I'm afraid that maybe his
8   mother has babied him so much that he doesn't want to
9   give up the good life at home! Why should he spend time
10 somewhere else? She does everything for him.
11   All he cares about is his guitar and his video games. The
12 boy is obsessed with them. I'm positive that he would never
13 leave his room if we didn't make him. Well, when I was his
14 age, we didn't sit around in our house all day! If I wasn't at
15 my friends' houses, I was at my girlfriend's. This kid never
16 leaves home!
17   He never uses the phone either. His girlfriend will call
18 and he'll be like, "Let me call you back." Then he never
19 does! It's no wonder he had over a thousand text messages
20 from her last month — it's the only way she can get a hold
21 of him! She's got to be ready to dump him! He never pays
22 a bit of attention to her. Surely this isn't how all the boys
23 act at school!
24   Don't get me wrong. It's not that I expect him — or want
25 him — to be out every night or tying up the phone twenty-
26 four-seven. I just want to make sure he's — you know — a
27 normal guy! Not *that guy* that holes up in his room, wears
28 a full-length trench coat, and goes to school with plans to
29 do God knows what!
30   Is it crazy that I actually want my pre-teen son to be
31 interested in girls? Maybe I'm the one who needs help!

Super-Stah!

(3 Girls)

93. TERRI'S VERSION
2

3   TERRI: You'd think — the way everyone is acting — that
4 Amber won a Grammy or something. Or maybe snagged a
5 spot on *America's Hottest Model.*
6   It was a stupid *mall* contest! Amber only won because
7 no one with any a shred of dignity would even enter such a
8 lame contest. It was basically a free plug for the clothing
9 stores. And has everyone forgotten the fact that the votes
10 were bought? That's right! A dollar a vote! So basically
11 Amber only won because my parents and grandparents were
12 willing to shell out some serious cash — just to see her get
13 the crown!
14   Now she's strutting around the house like a future Miss
15 America and Mom has gone completely crazy. All of a
16 sudden Amber needs an acting coach, a whole new
17 wardrobe, and a modeling class.
18   It's getting worse every day! I swear I saw Mom online
19 checking out real estate in Los Angeles! She thinks we're
20 going to have to move there so that Amber can "make a go
21 of it" and "get discovered!" Everyone around here has gone
22 star-struck, and she's nowhere close to being a star!
23   The last straw is the fact that I'm pretty sure Mom
24 borrowed from *my* college fund to pay for Amber to get head
25 shots! Well, I'm telling you one thing, if this doesn't blow
26 over soon, they won't be able to take those head shots
27 because her head will be too big to fit through the door!

1　　　　　　　94. AMBER'S VERSION

2

3　　　AMBER: O-M-G! My sister is *so* jealous of me right now!
4　She can hardly stand to be in the same room with me
5　because no one pays any attention to her any more!
6　Whenever she is around me, she's rolling her eyes or making
7　some sarcastic comment.

8　　　Ever since I won that modeling contest — I beat out
9　fourteen other girls, you know, so that has to tell you
10　something — my life has been a complete whirlwind. Head
11　shots. Modeling coach. Acting lessons. It's a dream come
12　true.

13　　　Mom is even thinking of moving to California so that I
14　can get discovered! Get a real acting gig! Become a famous
15　movie star! How amazing is that? No one could have better
16　parents than me.

17　　　I know it's causing issues between Terri and me, but
18　that's *her* problem. I don't know why she's so upset anyway
19　because she had her chance to be in the contest and she
20　snubbed her nose at it. Said it was the lamest thing she'd
21　ever seen. Well, how lame could it have been if all this has
22　happened because of it? Mom and Dad have finally seen my
23　potential! They're behind me all the way — which is way
24　more than I can say for Terri. She keeps acting like this is
25　just a phase and that nothing big is going to happen. She
26　can forget ever being in my acceptance speech at the
27　Oscars!

28　　　She's too small-minded to see that all great actresses
29　have to start somewhere — even if it *is* a mall contest!

1
2   95. MOTHER'S VERSION
3   MOTHER: Ever since I was a little girl, I've dreamed of
4 being a movie star. I even starred in two high school plays
5 and one community theatre play. But nothing ever came of
6 it. It was such a disappointment. Well, now one of my
7 daughters is going to become a big star! It's so exciting.
8 Seeing Amber get that crown placed on her head was one of
9 the most amazing moments of my life. I could just imagine
10 myself up there, smiling and waving. I know it's something
11 we'll both never forget!
12   This is just the beginning! Winning that mall contest is
13 going to open so many doors for Amber. I've always known
14 that she had that star quality, and now everyone else will,
15 too! But we have to strike while the iron is hot. Get her out
16 there now so that she can get noticed. There's just so much
17 to do! Head shots, modeling and acting classes! It's one
18 appointment after the other! Just organizing everything is
19 completely taking over my life!
20   But it will be worth every second. I'm willing to make the
21 sacrifice. I don't want to be one of those parents who was
22 unwilling to do whatever it takes — even if that means
23 packing up and moving! No hurdle is too big for my little girl!
24 I don't want any doors closed to Amber because of me.
25   It's been a little rough on our family. I think Terri is really
26 struggling with jealousy, so I've got to be sure and include
27 her in everything. I know she'll get on board with everything
28 when she sees how exciting it's going to be for everyone.
29 Who knows? Maybe she'll get bit by the acting or modeling
30 bug, too! Or ... maybe they'll need someone to play a
31 motherly role!

Do As I Do!

(2 Girls, 1 boy)

96. ROBIN'S VERSION

2

3   ROBIN: About six months ago my parents got this great
4 idea. They'd quit their respectable, decent-paying jobs and
5 open their very own hole-in-the-wall, suck-every-moment-
6 out-of-our-lives, restaurant. Do I sound bitter? Well, I am.
7 Far be it from me to stand in the way of their dreams. But
8 since when did their dream have to include me?
9   "It's a family business," they said, and then they put me
10 on their work schedule. My brother, too, and he's only
11 twelve! Every day after school I have to wait tables at their
12 stinking restaurant! Then I'm up until midnight or later
13 doing my homework! It's not fair! I did not sign up for this
14 family dream!
15   But lack of sleep isn't even the worst part. See, it's
16 actually a pretty hopping place — and my friends come
17 here! Let me be perfectly clear on this: I do *not* want to wait
18 on my friends. It's, like, so ... pathetic. One of them even
19 thought it'd be funny to whistle at me. Like a dog. *(Pause)*
20 Then I had to pay to get her clothes cleaned after I dumped
21 her plate of spaghetti on her. Now she's not even talking to
22 me! How come it was funny to whistle but not funny to wear
23 a plate of food on her head?
24   I'd quit — if they'd even let me — except that my
25 *brilliant* parents spent their life savings on this endeavor
26 and so, oops — there goes my college fund! This isn't a
27 dream, it's a nightmare! Didn't they remember that I have
28 dreams of my own? I want to go to school in New York City

1 and become a fashion designer. One so hot that I get to
2 snap and whistle at people so they come running to me! I do
3 not want to be a waitress at a crummy family restaurant!
4 *(Looks off to side.)* Yeah, I hear you. *(Rolls eyes.)* Food's up. I
5 gotta go.
6
7 **97. BROTHER'S VERSION**
8
9   BROTHER: My parents are so cool. They bought this old
10 run-down restaurant and turned it into the greatest place in
11 town! They let me work there and I'm only twelve years old!
12 They pay me, too. And sometimes if they're short-staffed I
13 get to wait on tables and then I get tips and I get to keep
14 them! I've got so much money saved up I can buy any video
15 game I want. In fact, I can buy a whole new system!
16   Another great thing is that they're so wrapped up in the
17 business, they've totally forgotten about schoolwork. I
18 hardly ever have to do homework any more. Mom and Dad
19 are always too tired to care about it by the time we get
20 home. They're way less focused on straight A's now. Their
21 new philosophy is that they're teaching me life skills instead.
22 If I play my cards right, they might let me quit school
23 completely!
24   Just kidding. I don't really want to quit school. But at
25 least I know I'll always have the family business to fall back
26 on when I get older and I won't have to worry about fighting
27 my sister for it! She absolutely hates the place! Personally I
28 think it's because she hates working. She always acts like
29 everything she has to do is so beneath her. What a princess.
30 She's lucky Mom and Dad even pay her. She doesn't work
31 half as hard as I do.
32   I really don't see what her problem is. There are worse
33 places she could have to work. And she gets to see her
34 friends all the time because all the kids from school come
35 here! What more could she possibly ask for?

1
2

98. MOTHER'S VERSION

3   MOTHER: My husband and I finally broke free of the
4   corporate world and started our own business! We took the
5   plunge, invested everything we had, and bought a
6   restaurant! It's been completely amazing! The best thing we
7   could've ever done to bond our family.
8   We couldn't have done it without everyone pitching in!
9   My mother works the hostess stand every lunch hour. My
10   husband's father handcrafted the salad bar. My nephew is
11   the fry cook, and my sister bakes homemade pies at home.
12   Best of all, we get to see our son and daughter every day
13   now! That's certainly a rarity with a pre-teen boy and a
14   teenage girl!
15   We used to work such hectic schedules that we hardly
16   ever sat down to dinner together. Most nights we saw our
17   kids just in time to tell them goodnight. Now we see each
18   other all the time. Oh, we may not get to eat together, but
19   we're around each other so much more than before. It's
20   been an amazing gift to my family. I wish we'd done this
21   years ago!
22   The kids are learning some great life skills here, too,
23   though Robin would never admit it. But I know she's
24   learning things she can take with her when she goes to high
25   school and off to college! *(Pause)* We've had a few issues, of
26   course, like the time she dumped food on one of her friends.
27   But she's really maturing! She hasn't had any bad comment
28   cards for over a month. Maybe she's finally taking ownership
29   of the place — which she should — because one day it will
30   all be hers and her brother's! She might not see it now, but
31   when she's older she will be so thankful to us for giving her
32   this incredible opportunity!

Low-Down Cheating Friend
(2 Guys, 1 girl)

1
2
3   JERRY: My life is like straight out of a country music
4 video. In fact, I'm almost positive there's a song that is
5 exactly like what's happened to me. How could I have been
6 so blind? So stupid? How could I have missed all the
7 sneaking around ... the muffled phone calls? The fact that
8 he had my sister's cell phone number in *his* cell phone!
9   That's right. You probably caught this faster than I did.
10 My best friend's cheating on me — with my little sister,
11 Tessa! How gross is that? All this time I thought he was
12 coming over here to hang out with me and all he wanted was
13 to get close to her! Do you have any idea how horrible it is
14 to open the door to your house and find your friend wrapped
15 around your sister? My eyes are still burning.
16   And so is my fist! Of course I hit him! You don't slobber
17 all over someone's sister and think you can get away with
18 it. He's two years older than she is. She's just a baby. Only
19 twelve years old! What was he thinking? What was *she*
20 thinking? I can't wait to tell Mom and Dad! They're going to
21 ground her for life. They'll never let her out of the house
22 again. She'll never be allowed to date. They'll probably
23 make her join a convent or something. Or go off to boarding
24 school. Kissing a boy like that — a boy she barely even
25 knows! At the innocent age of *twelve!* Well ... OK, maybe
26 she knows him because of me — I mean he practically lives
27 here ... and now we all know *why*, don't we?
28   What a scumbag! Taking advantage of me that way.

Worming his way into my life so he can flirt with my little
sister. He's lucky I only punched him once. If he hadn't
gotten out of here, I would've pulverized his face. When he
sees me coming down the hall, he'd better run the other
way. I never want to speak to him again!

100. ANDREW'S VERSION

ANDREW: My life is definitely worthy of being a soap
opera. It is. There I was, minding my own business, waiting
in my best friend's living room until he finished mowing the
lawn, when wham! In comes his little sister, Tessa and she
is H-O-T. Says she going outside to work on her tan. She's
wearing this skimpy halter-top thing and asks me to tie it
up in the back. Batting those eyes, telling me she can't
reach — when I know she can.

What could I do? Say no? Like I can't handle tying a
girl's shirt? So she stood in front of me — facing me — and
when I told her to turn around so I could see better, she
throws her arms around my neck and kisses me! Right as
my friend Jerry walks in!

I can imagine how it looked — and what he thought. He
didn't even give me a chance to explain. Just started
swinging at my face. I knew he was not in the mood to
listen, so I ran out of there. I'll call him later and after he
hears what happened, we'll both be laughing.

He has to know I would never look twice at Tessa — well,
OK, maybe I'd look at her ... I mean, she's definitely not the
scrawny little brat she used to be — but I would never want
to *be* with her. I don't know what got into her. Now I'm
afraid to go back over there. Who knows what she's going
to do? Especially now that she knows how upset Jerry got.
She'll do anything to taunt him.

Good thing Jerry knows me better than that. He knows
I would never touch his sister ... no matter what it looked

1   like ... wait a minute! Why isn't *he* calling *me* to apologize?

2   He's the one who hit me! Shouldn't he have figured things

3   out by now? What kind of a friend is he to think I would do

4   something like that? And to punch me without even hearing

5   my side of the story ... when I see him next, he'd better do

6   some fast-talking because if he doesn't grovel quickly, he's

7   going to be the one with the black eye!

8

9   101. TESSA'S VERSION

10

11   TESSA: You should've seen my brother's face! It was

12 absolutely priceless! I don't think he would've been more

13 shocked if he'd caught *Mom* in his best friend's arms! All

14 the color drained from his face, his mouth dropped open,

15 and his eyes got so big I thought they were going to pop out

16 of his head.

17   I don't even know how he moved across the room that

18 fast. If I wasn't so mad at him, I might even think that was

19 sweet. That he felt so protective of me that he actually

20 punched his best friend! Except that really just magnifies

21 why I'm mad at him in the first place! This just proves again

22 how he thinks I'm still a little girl that needs his protection!

23 He sees me as a baby, and I'm tired of it. I'm almost a

24 teenager!

25   Why can't he hang out with me sometimes? We're not

26 that far apart in age. But he thinks he is like an adult and

27 I'm just a kid. Know what he did the other day? Told my

28 parents that he would not spend his Friday night babysitting

29 me! *Babysitting me!* Like I'm too young to stay alone. They

30 didn't even ask him to. He found out that they were going to

31 be gone, and those were the first words out of his mouth,

32 "Well, don't expect me to babysit Tessa. I've got plans." He

33 is so full of himself.

34   So, yeah, I staged the whole thing with his friend so that

35 he would finally see me as the age I really am and not as

1   some snot-nosed kid with pigtails! I am old enough to like
2   boys and have boys like me, so he might as well get used to
3   it. I swear he's worse than Dad.
4   I just hope I didn't give Andrew the wrong idea — when
5   I do get a boyfriend, it definitely will *not* be him! Ewwww!
6   He's my brother's best friend! It's like we're practically
7   related!

About the Author

This is Rebecca Young's third book of monologues. Regarding her inspiration for the 300 plus monologues she's written so far, she says, "I have three girls; two of whom are still teenagers, one just barely out of that age range. It's all about comedy and tragedy around my house. Believe me, there's not much else in between." Friends and family (she won't dare say who), television, and just a plain old overactive imagination help Rebecca create a wide array of monologues to choose from.

When she's not writing monologues, Rebecca writes and directs drama for middle and high school students at her church. She co-founded a group called One Voice that travels annually to perform at various churches. It is a great passion of hers to combine writing and working with youth.

Rebecca currently works in a totally "non-dramatic" profession as a technical trainer in Lexington, Kentucky. She has a B.A. in Communications/Marketing from the University of Kentucky.

Ms. Young lives with her husband (Frank), three wonderful and dramatic daughters (Heather, Kristina, and Ashley), and two cats (who have names but are more often than not called Orange Kitty and Gray Kitty. And lately, "Bad Kitty" because one has been having issues!)

Whether you are an actor or a writer, she suggests this quote as a daily mantra: "You aren't finished when you lose; you are finished when you quit."